Global Issues Series

General Editor: **Jim Whitman**

This exciting new series encompasses three principal themes: the interaction of human and natural systems; cooperation and conflict; and the enactment of values. The series as a whole places an emphasis on the examination of complex systems and causal relations in political decision-making; problems of knowledge; authority, control and accountability in issues of scale; and the reconciliation of conflicting values and competing claims. Throughout the series the concentration is on an integration of existing disciplines towards the clarification of political possibility as well as impending crises.

Titles include:

Michael Pugh (*editor*)
REGENERATION OF WAR-TORN SOCIETIES

Bhaskar Vira and Roger Jeffery (*editors*)
ANALYTICAL ISSUES IN PARTICIPATORY NATURAL RESOURCE MANAGEMENT

Simon M. Whitby
BIOLOGICAL WARFARE AGAINST CROPS

Global Issues Series
Series Standing Order ISBN 0–333–79483–4
(*outside North America only*)

You can receive future titles in this series as they are published by placing a standing order. Please contact your bookseller or, in case of difficulty, write to us at the address below with your name and address, the title of the series and the ISBN quoted above.

Customer Services Department, Macmillan Distribution Ltd, Houndmills, Basingstoke, Hampshire RG21 6XS, England

Approaches to Peacebuilding

Edited by

Ho-Won Jeong

Associate Professor
Institute for Conflict Analysis and Resolution
George Mason University
Fairfax, USA

First published 2002 by
PALGRAVE MACMILLAN
Houndmills, Basingstoke, Hampshire RG21 6XS and
175 Fifth Avenue, New York, N.Y. 10010
Companies and representatives throughout the world

PALGRAVE MACMILLAN is the global academic imprint of the Palgrave
Macmillan division of St. Martin's Press, LLC and of Palgrave Macmillan Ltd.
Macmillan® is a registered trademark in the United States, United Kingdom
and other countries. Palgrave is a registered trademark in the European
Union and other countries.

ISBN 0–333–98192–8

This book is printed on paper suitable for recycling and made from fully
managed and sustained forest sources.

A catalogue record for this book is available from the British Library.

Library of Congress Cataloging-in-Publication Data
Approaches to peacebuilding / edited by Ho-Won Jeong.
        p. cm. — (Global issues series)
    Includes bibliographical references and index.
    ISBN 0–333–98192–8 (cloth)
        1. Peace. 2. Social engineering. 3. Peacekeeping forces. I. Jeong,
Ho-Won. II. Global issues series (Palgrave (Firm))

    JZ5538 .A675 2002
    303.6'9—dc21

                                                            2002072517

10   9   8   7   6   5   4   3   2   1
11   10 09 08 07 06 05 04 03 02

Printed and bound in Great Britain by
Antony Rowe Ltd, Chippenham and Eastbourne

Contents

Part IV Policy Design and Operational Issues

Preface

Over the last decade or so, there has been a growing demand for new knowledge about how divided societies can be transformed. Peacebuilding has become a particularly important subject as more countries move toward the stage of reconstructing their societies following communal violence. The Failure of peacebuilding in violence ridden societies can create not only national but also regional and international security problems, as is suggested by Afghanistan.

Post-conflict reconstruction and the prevention of future conflict has been one of the new agendas at foreign service agencies in Europe and the US as well as major international organisations such as the United Nations, the Organsation of Security and Cooperation in Europe, the European Union and NATO. Along with the establishment of post-conflict reconstruction units in many Western governments and international organizations, academic interest in rebuilding war torn societies has grown.

In the official policy making circle and associated research communities, the main goals of peacebuilding have been related to maintaining a liberal political order by containing and reducing the intensity, duration and geographic spill-over of violent conflict. Since controlling the spread of violence is considered important for the stability of the liberal international order, the diplomatic agendas are much consumed by how violence-prone societies can be integrated into a regional and international order through state building projects.

While benefiting from research accumulated in such areas as peacekeeping, reconciliation, elections, humanitarian aid and development assistance, this book intends to provide more integrative pictures of multiple dimensions of transition to a stable social order. In doing so, most importantly, this book contributes to an increased knowledge base in such ignored areas as policy design, operation and implementation.

Peacebuilding is understood in terms of multilevel decision making and operational processes. While the logistics for peace operations are still affected by strategic imperatives, development, reconciliation and other projects for social reconstruction cannot be fully addressed through negotiation at a political and diplomatic level. This volume treats peacebuilding operations as more than political and strategic considerations by adding the perspectives of communal security and conflict resolution reflecting on the concerns of local populations.

With its coverage of key conceptual and policy issues for peacebuilding, this edited book will broadly appeal to both research and policy making communities. It can be adopted by many advanced-level college and postgraduate courses in international relations as well as in the interdisciplinary field of peace and conflict studies. At the same time, policy makers can benefit from an analytical understanding of policy oriented issues.

In completing this project, I wish to express my intellectual debt to Chadwick F. Alger, John W. Burton, Elise Boulding and Johan Galtung. I also appreciate several experts who offered consultation or comments on various parts of the manuscript. In particular, my gratitude goes to Jurgen Dedring, Charles Lerche, Gustavo Gozzi, Hideaki Shinoda, Luc Reychler, Jessica Senehi and Sean Byrne. In addition, this book could not have moved forward much without the support of Jim Whitman whose intellect stimulated new thinking.

The fellowship awarded by the Government and Parliament of the Region Emilia-Romagna, Italy, in the summer of 2000, was pivotal to the development of the various agendas for this book. I am grateful to Jennifer Dougherty who produced the copy edited manuscript; Viveki Piscini, Channa Threat and Adina Friedman have also contributed to the editing. Finally, the support of Mary and Nimmy as well as my parents was most valuable in completing this book project.

Notes on the Contributors

Charles-Philippe David is the Teleglobe-Raould Dandurand Chair of Strategic and Diplomatic Studies and Professor of Political Science at University of Quebec in Montreal. He has extensively published in French and English on topics related to peace missions, American foreign and defense policies, and security issues in general.

Ho-Won Jeong is Associate Professor for the Institute for Conflict Analysis and Resolution, George Mason University. His current research areas include structural sources of conflict, social change, and peacebuilding. Dr. Jeong published a series on research in peace and conflict studies comprised of *The New Agenda for Peace Research* (1999), *Conflict Resolution: Dynamics, Process and Structure* (1999), and *Peace and Conflict Studies: An Introduction* (2000) in addition to many journal articles. He is Senior Editor of *International Journal of Peace Studies* (published in association with the International Peace Research Association's Commissions) and Editor-in-Chief of *Peace and Conflict Studies* (sponsored by the Network of Peace and Conflict Studies).

David Last teaches in the Department of Political Science at the Royal Military College of Canada. Dr. Last served on peacekeeping missions in Cyprus, Croatia, and Bosnia. He has extensively written on peacekeeping and peacebuilding as an associate for the Pearson Peacekeeping Centre.

Charles Lerche is Associate Professor of Political Science at Vesalius College, Vrije Universirteit Brussel, an adjunct faculty member of the University of Kent at Canterbury's Brussels School of International Studies, and Gastdocent at the University of Limburg/Maastricht, the Netherlands. His research interests include international relations, the politics of the Global South, world order, peace and conflict studies, and Bahai Studies. He co-authored *Concepts of International Politics in Global Perspective*, edited two volumes of essays on world order studies, and published articles in several academic journals, including *The Journal of African Studies*, *Journal of Asian and African Studies*, *Peace and Conflict Studies*, *The International Journal of Peace Studies*, and *Journal of Bahai Studies*.

Susan McKay is a professor of nursing, women's and international studies at the University of Wyoming and a psychologist in private practice. She is past president of the Division of Peace Psychology of the American Psychological Association. Her awards include the Year 2000 Presidential Award for research from the University of Wyoming, U.S. West Excellence in Education, Woman of Achievement from the Wyoming Commission for Women, and DePauw University's Alumni Citation. She was awarded fellowships from the W.K. Kellogg Foundation and the International Federation of University Women and was selected as a scholar in residence at the Rockefeller Foundation's Bellagio Center in Italy. She has published over 40 journal articles, book chapters and three books.

Bertram I. Spector is Executive Director of the Center for Negotiation Analysis. Dr. Spector is currently completing a book on post-agreement negotiations and international regimes. He is also Editor-in-Chief of *International Negotiation*. In the past, he directed the Processes of International Negotiation (PIN) Project at the International Institute for Applied Systems Analysis in Laxenburg, Austria. He was also a Fellow at the Foreign Policy Institute of the Paul Nitze School of Advanced International Studies (SAIS) at the Johns Hopkins University from 1993-95.

Part I: Introduction

1 Peacebuilding: Conceptual and Policy Issues

Ho-Won Jeong

Difficult peace negotiations can create the conditions necessary for the settlement of intrastate violence and war in many divided societies. This book focuses on diverse processes and strategies for the transition from violent conflict to post-conflict reconstruction. In order to obtain a peace settlement that is durable, 'institutions and support structures must be put in place so that the parties are discouraged from taking up arms again' (Hampson, 1996, pp. 9-10). In investigating a post-settlement situation, thus, it is important to identify actions and support structures that will prevent a relapse into violent conflict. The volume explores the ways dynamics of post-conflict situations can be transformed for the achievement of sustainable peace.

More specifically, this edited volume is designed to provide a conceptual understanding of various approaches to security, development and social rehabilitation. In doing so, it attempts to narrow the gap between theory and practice relevant to the transformation of violent structures. Reflecting on this theme, the contributors assess various strategies for peacebuilding, and analyse their conceptual assumptions and policy objectives. The chapters focus on designs and models of peacebuilding, multiple roles and functions of peacekeeping, capacity building through negotiation, reconciliation, and policy co-ordination among different components of peacebuilding.

Challenges

The general nature of peacebuilding can be characterised by the overwhelming demand for reconstructing societies crippled by serious long-term conflict. While it is an enormous task to bring adversarial parties to the negotiation table and reach an agreement, it is also an equally formidable task to ensure that the parties maintain their commitment to abiding by the process to which they agreed. Some peace settlements contributed to ending hostilities and violence, but there are other cases that have been unraveled by renewed fighting. The long civil war in Angola, which had its roots in the struggle for independence from Portugal in 1975, suggests how difficult it is to achieve stability when one of the adversarial parties decides to abandon peace agreements.

A peacebuilding process is based on the commitment of warring parties to resolve future conflict in political, not military, terms. For instance, the lack of a commitment from the Khmer Rouge destabilised the process of reconstruction in Cambodia. Thus, the control of destructive forces such as the Khmer Rouge has been an important issue in the Cambodian peace process. Rules and strategies for rebuilding a community are different from those of wartime when planning is inevitably focused on the immediate survival. Concrete packages of mutual commitments and undertakings have to follow the initial agreement to peace. Their commitments will be weak if former adversaries do not take enough stake in the peace process. External support can play a critical role in preventing a fragile peace process from breaking down.

Dynamics

The transition from peace making to peacebuilding is not necessarily linear given that the negotiated settlement of a long-term conflict brings about new challenges as well as opportunities for transformation of conflict relationships (Jeong, 1999). Policy implementation can be hampered by political fragmentation and systemic crisis. The warring factions do not suddenly change their behaviour after peace agreements. The implementation of the peace agreement is often delayed by continuing mutual mistrust. For instance, the lack of progress in the El Salvador government land transfer programme halted a phased disarmament by opposition rebel forces in October 1992. The terms of settlement are often renegotiated during the implementation process, as foot-dragging practices and broken promises are common.

Peace agreements are not the end of old conflict because they do not by themselves provide a guarantee for successful implementation. The stated goals of the agreements often reflect compromised solutions at the negotiation table. Parties may well find out that implementing the agreement does not best serve their interests. As we have recently seen in the Israeli-Palestinian conflict, the escalating spiral of alleged violations and retaliation unravelled the entire peace process. Thus the task remains to build mutual confidence among former adversaries to reduce the risk of turning to renewed hostilities and violent battles.

As conflict is not a static process, peacebuilding has its own challenges. Many protracted conflicts are locked in vicious cycles of confrontation characterised by social divisions along ethnic, religious, and class lines (Jeong, 2000). These divisions affect the outcome of efforts to reverse self-sustaining patterns of hostilities and violence. The dynamics of peacebuilding are related to changes in ongoing human interactions and perceptions. At the same time, transforming the nature of intrastate conflict would not be easy without directly changing a social and political environment that continues to engender adversarial relationships.

Processes

Post-settlement activities are associated with the establishment of a comprehensive and durable process to implement a peace agreement. Peace making is designed to enable hostile parties to find compromised solutions by such means as mediation and negotiation. On the other hand, peacebuilding is directly related to laying down a foundation for social harmony supported by measures which foster cooperation among adversarial communities. Social, political, and economic infrastructures have to be developed to prevent future violence. Negotiated peace making is not a separate process from peacebuilding. Ambiguities in an agreement have to be resolved in the process of implementation.

Since the existence of on-going problems requires continued negotiation, a peace process needs to be extended to set up political solutions for the existing tensions in society. Group facilitation and mediation can support direct negotiations between opposing parties at both national and local levels. As happened in the post-conflict settlement of several Central American countries, national and local peace commissions comprised of various factions can oversee the implementation of peace accords. Due to a low level of trust between former adversaries, third party facilitation helps overcome a climate of mutual distrust and suspicion (Lederach, 1994). Implementing the agreement needs to be supervised, monitored, or assisted through the presence of international observers.

The process of peacebuilding is comprised of various functions and roles. Peacebuilding entails a wide range of sequential activities from demobilisation of paramilitary groups and other security arrangements to refugee resettlement, economic reconstruction and the advancement of human rights. Following the accomplishment of negotiated agreement, the management of humanitarian crisis situations turns into community building activities. Peacebuilding involves both short-term responses to various crisis situations and social instability as well as long-term visions for reconstruction (Jeong, 2001). Short-term management plans are based on intense negotiations to overcome volatile situations and respond to the immediate needs of returning refugees and the displaced as well as a lack of public services for local residents. Essential government functions that provide basic social services have to be immediately restored. Most settlement agreements have a timetable for a cease-fire, the subsequent demobilisation of armed combatants, and local and national elections.

A foundation for creating stable relations between communities can be laid through efforts to rebuild political, economic and social structures of the war-torn societies. Such peacebuilding strategies as promotion of national reconciliation, social and economic improvement, reform in state institutions and political representation are aimed at reducing socioeconomic cleavages and regional animosities. Thus the end of violent conflict has to be accompanied by significant changes in socio-economic institutions beyond the maintenance of cease-fire, disarmament and participation of former adversaries in a formal, democratic political process.

Recreating political institutions is a crucial task for maintaining stability in failed states such as Liberia, Somalia, and Afghanistan where civil wars have destroyed the foundations of both governmental and civic institutions. In promoting interdependent communal relations, development programmes have to be designed to address economic inequities and social disparities that are the root causes of violence. A participatory process associated with empowerment and trust building helps achieve the long-term goals of sustainable economies and self-governance (Bloomfield, 1989). What has happened in the past needs to be confronted in order to heal a fractured community, and the parameters of peacebuilding will be eventually tested by the possibilities of transformative relationships. The goals of peacebuilding are achieved by reconstruction and reconciliation, which are essential to the prevention of future conflict.

Institutional Transformation

Peacebuilding is based on the expectation that long-term security interests are served by the promotion of a just society. An appropriate social environment has to be created to allow identity groups to express their needs and grievances in a constructive manner. Durable peace is not possible without guaranteeing procedural and distributive justice. Peacebuilding can be characterised by 'a long term preventive strategy aimed at tackling the root causes of conflict' (Peck, 1996, p. 74).

With the recognition of a powerful trend toward democratisation, the notion of 'neoliberal peacebuilding' (characterised by the establishment of formal democratic procedures combined with the promotion of market economies) has been universally applied. Liberal democratic visions stress formal institutions and rules as well as political representation through elections (Lipschutz, 1998; Parris, 1997). Thus, reform for democratic institution building mostly focuses on creating formal rules for political competition. In the application of the Western theoretical tradition of democratisation to post-conflict societies, however, more serious attention needs to be paid to the substantive outcomes of a competitive political process. Strategies for building democratic institutions have to be adaptable to a specific context of local culture and political traditions.

Institutional transformation has to be geared toward addressing deeper political and social causes and consequences of communitarian violence. The approaches in this volume attempt to overcome the shortcomings of the existing approaches, which consider a peacebuilding process largely formal and presents it as a largely technical tasks comprised of setting up government institutions and providing judicial and other services. Elections and other formal democratic mechanisms have to be introduced in a way that will directly deal with power imbalance among groups. In order to enhance social harmony, the emphasis of economic recovery lies in the distributional aspects of macro economic policies. Institutional approaches mostly aimed toward re-establishing the rules of state governance (without questioning the substantive outcome of the political process) do not eliminate structural conditions of violent conflict associated with inequity and marginalisation.

Formal institutionalisation of a political process does not necessarily guarantee genuine expression of people's interests if the process is dominated by a few who monopolise resources for political mobilisation. Stability of a multi-party system relies on the related features of an economic and social structure such as a healthy civil society (based on the existence of a middle class). As seen in the case of Liberia, the legitimation of power of a former warlord by victory in the national elections can result in forced consent and oppression of opponents.

Assessment

Due to continuing challenges and questions, the issues of peacebuilding operations need to be more fully and further investigated. This edited volume aims to fill the gap created by the insufficiency in conceptual knowledge and a demand for more sophisticated policy responses that can guide the overall process of peacebuilding. The conceptual framework illustrated in this book can be applicable not only to societies which have been successful in restoring relatively stable relations between former adversaries (for example, Mozambique, El Salvador, and Namibia) but also to societies whose reconstruction efforts have not yet produced hopeful signs (for example, Bosnia, Kosovo, and Somalia).

Research on peacebuilding is mostly based on single or comparative case studies in Cambodia, Somalia, Angola, Ethiopia, Mozambique, Namibia, Liberia, South Africa, Haiti, El Salvador, Guatemala, Nicaragua and other countries (Anstee, 1996; Arnson, 1999; Baregu, 1999; Bariagaber, 1998; Chan and Vanancio, 1998; Holiday and Stanley, 1993; Knife and Tekel-Mikael, 1997; Kumar, 1998; Lincoln and Sereseres, 2000; Lisee, 2000; Marks, 2000; Menkhause, 1998). In terms of domains of research, diverse types of topics have been covered, ranging from ending civil wars (Licklider, 1993) to peacekeeping (Gordon and Toase, 2001; Ratner, 1995; Whitman, 1999); from elections (Kumar, 1998; Reilly and Reynolds, 2000) and political transition (Griffiths, 1998; Reychler, 1999) to reconciliation (Amadiume and Abdullahi, 2000; Biggar, 2001; Hayner, 2001; Kriesberg, 1999; Nigel, 2001; Rotberg and Thompson, 2000); and from development assistance (Boyce, 1996; Carbonnier, 1998) to gender and rehabilitation (Date-Bah and Walsh, 2001; McKay, 2000; Sorenson, 1998). While these studies help us understand various characteristics of different peace operations, our understanding will be incomplete without a more systematic approach to an overall process of peacebuilding.

Some research takes short-term crisis intervention approaches with an extensive focus on emergency relief and control of violence. Conflict management efforts, such as peacekeeping, need to be linked to a longer-term process of not only transforming the psychological environment of conflict but also social change. By illustrating interdependence of various elements of peacebuilding roles, this book attempts to help accomplish a more thorough examination of the complex aspects of peacebuilding.

The status of the field is at the stage of identifying the essential pieces of the puzzle to rebuild divided societies recovering from communal violence (Alger, 2000). The challenge remains how to deepen knowledge about the potential contributions of each piece while attempting to discern how the various strategies fit together. This book meets the challenges of providing an integrative peacebuilding model with the assessment of the past achievement and existing trends.

Overview

In one way or another, the following chapters of this book examine social, psychological and political factors that play an important role in success or failure of initiatives to bring about peace. Some chapters have been more thoroughly devoted to a social context of reconciliation and gender empowerment while others concentrate on such topics as operational and strategic issues for peacekeeping and negotiation.

It is important to survey major assumptions, objectives, and conditions under which peacebuilding proceeds and has been implemented. Understanding the effectiveness of different elements of peacebuilding is enhanced by examining how security, political, social, and economic components support each other in rebuilding the fabric of divided societies. The analysis in the book illustrates past and current experiences of peacebuilding and suggests conceptual and policy approaches that can overcome the weaknesses of existing strategies.

Following this chapter, Charles-Philippe David evaluates a neoliberal peacebuilding model. Difficulties and contradictions arising in the application of a liberal vision of democratic peacebuilding are explained in terms of the failure of post-conflict states to guarantee individual liberties and represent the collective will. The application of market democracy on a wider scale would be perilous in the absence of rigorous analysis of the model's impact on social and economic conditions. After examining the empirical scope of the concept of peacebuilding, the author concludes that expectations of peacebuilding need to scale down, and the process of democratisation must be controlled to be adaptable to local situations. Part II consists of peacekeeping and capacity building. Ho-Won Jeong's chapter sheds light on various functions of peacekeeping and internal operational issues as well as an external political environment. This chapter looks for various ways short-term peacekeeping contributes to a long-term transition of peacebuilding interventions. Peacekeeping is understood in terms of a framework for third party roles in maintaining security, restoring public order and community building.

The implementation of policy change cannot proceed efficiently in an atmosphere marked by excessive or disruptive conflict. Thus, a necessary condition of implementing policy change effectively must be the design, development, and institutionalisation of processes and structures that are capable of managing, if not resolving, disputes that threaten policy reform. At the same time, countries undergoing such periods of policy change and uncertainty often lack the capacity to respond effectively to conflict and may lack the will to react to conflict altogether. The chapter 'Negotiation Readiness in the Development Context: Adding Capacity to Ripeness' by Betram Spector seeks to understand the centrality of the concept of negotiation readiness for successful development and peacebuilding efforts.

The main issues discussed in Part III are reconciliation and gender in peacebuilding. In the main body of the chapter, 'Reconciliation: Contexts and Consequences', Charles Lerche and Ho-Won Jeong see reconciliation as a process and a condition. They review shortcomings of psychological approaches and suggest political strategies for reconciliation. In the concluding section, they argue that if the process towards reconciliation is to be sustained, then it must be deepened and grounded in social justice.

In her chapter 'Gender and Post-Conflict Reconstruction', Susan McKay presents the view that post-conflict reconstruction most often focuses upon rebuilding of institutions and structures with scant acknowledgement made to how war-ending, reconciliation and rebuilding processes are profoundly gendered. The theme of this chapter is that when societies are reconstructing, conflict exists between the exigencies of nationalism and achievement of women's equality; nationalistic loyalties are more highly valued than gender equality. By using a feminist perspective, the author discusses gendered processes of reconstruction, justice and reconciliation.

Part IV examines peacebuilding designs and operational issues. Ho-Won Jeong's chapter on peacebuilding design presents a synergetic model in which various policy components interact with each other to maximise their effects on the outcome. Conditions for the success or failure of peacebuilding have to be assessed in terms of a coherent action plan to help a given population move from the status of extreme vulnerability and dependency to that of self-sufficiency and well-being. This chapter looks at not only objective but also subjective environments that enhance or prohibit transition to a sustainable peace. Most importantly, it also develops conceptual tools needed to assess the impact of different kinds of intervention measures on the conflict transformation. More effective peacebuilding policies have to consider timing, priority setting, and other conditions that are relevant to intervention for peacebuilding.

The chapter by Ho-Won Jeong and David Last examines not only organisational issues for effective peacebuilding activities but also co-ordination among various actors at different levels. In successful peacebuilding operations, top-down approaches of international agencies need to be harmonised with bottom-up community building approaches. The chapter finds that non-governmental organisations can complement major international actors at both operational and tactical levels.

New conceptual understanding can be forged by examining functional relationships between different aspects of peacebuilding in complex situations that involve multiple actors with diverse demands. In this book, various conditions for social and institutional changes are examined, and strategies to overcome destabilising social effects and obstacles to reconciliation and reconstruction are explored.

REFERENCES

C. Alger, 'Challenges for Peace Researchers and Peace Builders in the Twenty-First Century', *International Journal of Peace Studies*, vol. 5, no. 1 (Spring 2000), pp. 1-13.

I. Amadiume and A. Abdullahi (eds), *The Politics of Memory: Truth, Healing and Social Justice* (New York: Zed Books, 2000).

M. J. Anstee, *Orphan of the Cold War: The Inside Story of the Collapse of the Angolan Peace Process* (New York: St. Martin's Press, 1996).

C. J. Arnson (ed.), *Comparative Peace Processes in Latin America* (Washington D.C.: Woodrow Wilson Center Press, 1999).

M. L. Baregu, *Preventive Diplomacy and Peace-Building in Southern Africa* (Harare, Zimbabwe: SAPES Trust, 1999).

A. Bariagaber, 'The Politics of Cultural Pluralism in Ethiopia and Eritrea: Trajectories of Ethnicity and Constitutional Experiments', *Ethnic and Racial Studies*, vol. 21, no. 6 (November 1998), pp. 1056-1073.

N. Biggar (ed.), *Burying the Past: Making Peace and Doing Justice after Civil Conflict* (Washington, D.C.: Georgetown University Press, 2001).

L. P. Bloomfield, 'Coping with Conflict in the Late Twentieth Century', *International Journal* (Autumn 1989).

B. Boutros-Ghali, *An Agenda for Peace: Preventive Diplomacy, Peacemaking and Peace-Keeping* (New York: United Nations, 1992), http://www.un.org/Docs/SG/agpeace.html.

J. Boyce (ed.), *Economic Policy for Building Peace: The Lessons of El Salvador* (Boulder: Lynn Rienner, 1996).

G. Carbonnier, 'Conflict, Postwar Rebuilding and the Economy: A Critical Review of the Literature', *War-Torn Societies Project Occasional Paper,* no. 2 (Geneva: UNRISD, 1998).

S. Chan and M. Vanancio (eds), *War and Peace in Mozambique* (New York: St. Martins Press, 1998).

E. Date-Bah and M. Walsh, *Gender and Armed Conflicts: Challenges for Decent Work, Gender Equity and Peace Building Agendas and Programmes* (Geneva: ILO, 2001).

D. S. Gordon and F. H. Toase (eds), *Aspects of Peacekeeping* (London: Frank Cass, 2001).

A. L. Griffiths (ed.), *Building Peace and Democracy in Post-Conflict Societies* (Halifax: Center for Foreign Policy Studies, Dalhousie University, 1998).

F. O. Hampson, *Nurturing Peace: Why Peace Settlements Succeed or Fail* (Washington, D.C.: United States Institute of Peace, 1996).

P. Harris and B. Reilly, *Electoral Systems and Conflict in Divided Societies*, National Academic Papers on International Conflict Resolution, no. 2 (Washington, D.C.: 1999).

P. Hayner, *Unspeakable Truths: Confronting State Terror and Atrocity* (New York: Routledge, 2001).

K. Henrard and S. Smis, 'Recent Experiences in South Africa and Ethiopia to Accommodate Cultural Diversity: A Regained Interest in the Right of Self-determination', *Journal of African Law*, vol. 44, no. 1 (2000), pp. 17-51.

D. Holiday and W. Stanley, 'Building the Peace: Preliminary Lessons from El Salvador', *Journal of International Affairs*, vol. 46 (Winter 1993), pp. 415-438.

H. W. Jeong, *Peace Building in Post-Conflict Societies: Processes and Strategies*, Published by Department of International Relations (Italy: Government of the Region Emilia-Romagnia, Spring 2001).

H.W. Jeong, *Peace and Conflict Studies: An Introduction* (Aldershot: Ashgate Publishing, 2000).

H. W. Jeong, 'Research on Conflict Resolution', in Ho-Won Jeong (ed.), *Conflict Resolution: Dynamics, Process and Structure* (Aldershot: Ashgate Publishing, 1999).

D. C. Jett, *Why Peacekeeping Fails* (New York: St. Martin's Press, 2000).

A. Knife and M.Tekle-Mikael, 'Report on the High-Level Symposium on Conflicts in Africa: Road to Nation-Building in the Post-Conflict Period' (Addis Ababa: Ethiopian International Institute for Peace and Development, 1997).

L. Kriesberg, 'Path to Varieties of International Reconciliation', in H. W. Jeong (ed.), *Conflict Resolution: Dynamics, Process and Structure* (Aldershot: Ashgate Publishing, 1999), pp. 105-130.

C. Kumar, *Building Peace in Haiti* (Boulder: Lynne Reinner, 1998).

K. Kumar, 'Postconflict Elections and International Assistance' in K. Kumar (ed.), *Postconflict Elections, Democratization, and International Assistance* (Boulder: Lynne Rienner, 1998), pp. 5-14.

J. P. Lederach, *Building Peace: Sustainable Reconciliation in Divided Societies* (Tokyo: UN University Press, 1994).

R. Licklider (ed.), *Stopping the Killing* (New York: New York University Press, 1993).

J. K. Lincoln and C. Sereseres, 'Resettling the Contras: the OAS Verification Commission in Nicaragua', in T. S. Montgomery (ed.), *Peacemaking and Democratization in the Western Hemisphere* (Coral Gables: North-South Center Press, University of Miami, 2000).

R. D. Lipschutz, 'Beyond the Neoliberal Peace: From Conflict Resolution to Social Reconciliation', *Social Justice*, vol. 25, no. 4 (Winter 1998), pp. 5-19.

P. P. Lizee, *Peace, Power and Resistance in Cambodia: Global Governance and the Failure of International Conflict Resolution* (New York: St. Martin's Press, 1999).

S. C. Marks, *Watching the Wind: Conflict Resolution During South Africa's Transition to Democracy* (Washington, D.C.: United States Institute of Peace Press, 2000).

S. McKay, 'Gender Justice and Reconciliation,' *Women's Studies International Forum*, vol. 25, no. 5 (2000).

K. Menkhause, 'Somalia: Political Order in a Stateless Society,' *Current History* (May 1998), pp.220-224.

R. Parris, 'Peacebuilding and the Limits of Liberal Internationalism,' *International Security*, vol. 22, no. 2 (Fall 1997), pp. 54-89.

C. Peck, *Sustainable Peace* (Lanham: Rowman & Littlefield, 1998).

S. R. Ratner, *The New UN Peacekeeping: Building Peace in Lands of Conflict After the Cold War* (Basingstoke: Macmillan, 1995).

B. Reilly and A. Reynolds, 'Electoral Systems and Conflict in Divided Societies', in P. Stern and D. Druckman (eds), *International Conflict Resolution after the Cold War* (Washington, D.C.: National Academy Press, 2000), pp. 420-482.

L. Reychler, *Democratic Peace-Building and Conflict Prevention: The Devil is in the Transition* (Leuven: Leuven University Press, 1999).

R. Rotberg and D. Thompson (eds), *Truth vs. Justice: The Morality of Truth Commissions* (Princeton: Princeton University Press, 2000).

R. L. Rothstein (ed.), *After the Peace: Resistance & Reconciliation* (Boulder: Lynne Rienner, 1999).

B. Sorenson, *Women and Post-Conflict Reconstruction* (Geneva: United Nations Research Institute for Social Development, 1998).

J. Whitman (ed.), *Peacekeeping and the UN Agencies* (London: Frank Cass, 1999).

2 Does Peacebuilding Build Peace?

Charles-Philippe David

It is the promise, not the perils, of peacebuilding that compels caution. (Bertram, 1995, p. 387)

Peacebuilding is one of the popular concepts underpinning United Nations (UN) missions today. Like other notions that have emerged since the end of the Cold War, particularly in connection with UN peace operations, 'peacebuilding' has become common currency. Peacebuilding is an ambitious concept that enjoys wide support. In general terms the concept pertains to the rehabilitation of regions and countries ravaged by armed conflicts in order to prevent the resumption of hostilities and to establish lasting peace. In 1997 four UN missions and one NATO mission pursued objectives related to peacebuilding (International Institute of Strategic Studies, 1997, pp. 274-284): in Angola, Haiti, Eastern Slovenia (Croatia),[1] and two complementary missions in Bosnia.[2] Since the end of the Cold War and with the expanding need for international peacekeeping forces, over a dozen UN missions have included peacebuilding functions, ranging from security tasks (disarmament, demobilisation, monitoring compliance with peace agreements, police training) to political assignments (supervision of elections, administration of justice, rebuilding the political system) and socio-economic missions (repatriation of refugees, bank reform, rebuilding roads, reviving agriculture). The United Nations and a wide variety of governmental and non-governmental organisations have been working for a dozen years to build peace around the world: in Namibia, Mozambique, Somalia, Rwanda, Nicaragua, Guatemala, El Salvador and Cambodia (in addition to the countries we have already mentioned).[3]

18

These post-Cold War missions are deemed to be more promising than those previously undertaken by the UN (such as the UN mission in the Congo between 1960 and 1963, which was a precursor to the idea of 'state-building') (Ruggie, 1996, p. 68). Freed from geopolitical stalemates and ideological rivalries, present circumstances are apparently more conducive to the acceptance and export of the liberal vision in which the concept of peacebuilding is grounded.[4] However, the reality is often quite different. Experience to date raises a number of questions to which the application of this new concept does not always supply adequate answers. It is disturbing to note that the solutions proposed and implemented can indeed aggravate rather than alleviate the problems addressed. It is the thesis of this paper that the concept of peacebuilding holds out much promise, but also many risks that must be carefully weighed before blindly applying the liberal premises, which brings this concept to bear upon conflict resolution and the promotion of peace.

What does the concept of peacebuilding mean? What distinguishes it from other concepts? What does it consist of in theory and in practice? What criteria can be drawn from analysis that would help determine the concept's suitability to a particular mission? These questions guide the following three-part discussion. First, we examine and discuss problems of definition. Secondly, we relate the concept to liberal theory on security. Finally, we examine the empirical scope of the concept and note difficulties and contradictions resulting from its application. By way of conclusion, certain useful criteria are proposed for evaluating prospects for success in future applications of the concept. This paper presents a conceptual and empirical overview rather than a study of specific peacebuilding situations, and as such it serves as an introduction to a new field of study that is in a constant process of development.

THE CONCEPT OF PEACEBUILDING

Like many others, the concept of peacebuilding is elastic. It may be broadly or narrowly defined, and there is no agreement on precise parameters among writers and documents that use the term, complicating conceptualisation. The recognised origin of the concept is found in the 1992 and 1995 editions of *An Agenda for Peace,* proposed by then-UN Secretary General Boutros Boutros-Ghali. Proclaiming the advent of a new generation of peace missions in the post-Cold War era, Boutros-Ghali suggested the use of innovative concepts such as peacebuilding, which he defined in 1992 as 'action to identify and support structures which will tend to strengthen and solidify peace in order to avoid a relapse into conflict' (Boutros-Ghali, 1992, p. 46). Such action can take several forms: demilitarisation, restructuring, police and judicial reform, economic development, elections, and so on. This very broad concept was subsequently used in 1995 in relation to two types of peacebuilding: efforts to reinforce preventive diplomacy (to remedy the root causes of conflict) and efforts to buttress peacemaking (institutionalising peace) (Boutros-Ghali, 1995, pp. 19-20).

Other writers, declarations and documents have attempted to circumscribe the concept by underscoring some of its specific aspects. Thus peacebuilding has been deemed to be synonymous with: 'reconciliation' (Love, 1995); 'cooperation among the parties to a conflict' (Lund, 1996, p. 400); 'attempting to build better relations' (Galtung, 1985, p. 151); 'casting a life line to foundering societies' (Minister Axworthy, 1996, p. 7); 'the practical implementation of peaceful social change' (Harbottle, 1984); 'the rebuilding of the institutions of the civil society' (Heininger, 1994); 'democratisation [as its] primary goal' (Canadian Center for Foreign Policy Development, 1996, p. 13); 'the effort to restore the capacity to work towards common security' (Regher, 1995); 'the promotion of human security in societies in conflict' (Cockell, 1997, p. 1); 'the creating of an environment to forestall the recurrence of conflict' (Open-Ended Working Group on an Agenda for Peace, June 10, 1996); and 'the full array of processes, approaches, and stages needed to transform conflict toward more sustainable, peaceful relationships' (Lederach, 1997, p. 20). The list of elastic definitions could easily be expanded, there being as many visions of peacebuilding as there are experts on the issue and actors in the field.

In general terms, three elements are central to the concept of peacebuilding, as it is understood: (1) the rehabilitation, reconstruction and reconciliation of societies that have suffered the ravages of armed conflict; (2) the creation of the security-related, political and/or socio-economic mechanisms needed to build trust between the parties and prevent the resumption of violence; (3) an external (foreign) intervention (national, multilateral or UN) to help create conditions conducive to peace. Beyond these elements, however, the debates surrounding the meaning of peacebuilding highlight a number of ambiguities.

1) Should peacebuilding be closely tied to development strategies? There are two currents of thought on the issue. They represent 'ideal types' between which writers often adopt qualified, intermediate positions. According to the 'exclusivist' school, these two dissimilar concepts should not be intertwined: peacebuilding is undertaken in response to security problems for a limited period of time, while development is a long-term strategy that is carried out under generally peaceful conditions.[5] In the 'exclusivist' view, a peacebuilding operation is confined to a two- to three-year period. The 'inclusivists', on the other hand, argue that development underlies the philosophy of peacebuilding, and that the latter cannot ultimately succeed unless it is integrated into a development initiative (and not the opposite).[6] On this basis, they maintain that peace missions should be conducted over longer periods of time (seven to eight years). While most experts recognise that the two concepts are interdependent, there is general agreement that peacebuilding embraces a much narrower range of situations (and study subjects) than development, and moreover is conducted in a context where security problems exist.

2) When are peacebuilding operations to be conducted? Once again, there are two schools of thought. The 'gradualists' hold that peacebuilding should generally be the last step after a political settlement has been reached, peace has been established ('peacemaking'), and a cease-fire agreed upon and observed ('peacekeeping') or, if need be, imposed ('peace-enforcement').[7] The 'synergists', on the other hand, maintain that peacebuilding efforts should be considered complementary to and supportive of other approaches such as preventive diplomacy before a conflict flares up or at any stage in the course of a peace mission (Fisher, 1993).

According to this school, peacebuilding benefits and contributes to peacekeeping, peacemaking and peace enforcement. In conjunction with these peace missions, peacebuilding seeks to attain reconciliation through a strategy of transformation (Lederach, 1997, pp. 73-85). Most observers believe that peacebuilding is more readily applicable after a civil war or conflict (hence the occasional use of the expression 'post-conflict peacebuilding'). However, the two outlooks are not incompatible insofar as, in practice, peace missions are frequently multidimensional in nature, and require the performance of all stages in an integrated manner. Indeed, peacebuilding can be conducted before, during, and after other related measures.

3) Does peacebuilding require that the parties to a conflict give their full consent prior to initiating a mission? According to the 'exclusivists' and the 'gradualists', such consent is usually an indispensable condition for the success and effectiveness of the mission—a condition without which the mission would be exposed to serious security problems.[8] The 'inclusivists' and 'synergists', on the other hand, do not necessarily make consent a prerequisite, since it is entirely possible in their view to contemplate an integrated peace mission, the objectives of which simultaneously include peacemaking, peacekeeping or even peace enforcement. All recognise that peacebuilding is more effective after the cessation of hostilities. It could, however, start as soon as diplomatic and military efforts are initiated to prevent or end an armed conflict. In short, consent could be by-passed but not without some risk.

4) By whom should peacebuilding operations be carried out? Again, for the 'exclusivists' and the 'gradualists', peacebuilding tasks should fall principally to civilians, in cooperation with the military, while the 'inclusivists' and the 'synergists' believe it may occasionally be necessary to entrust the military with some of the urgent peacebuilding tasks in the event that conditions remain dangerous on the ground. Furthermore, there is a more important debate between supporters of the UN and its institutions and representatives of NGOs with respect to the choice of civilian actors for peacebuilding (Weiss and Gordenker, 1996). The issue is crucial insofar as it raises the entire problem of coherence among the

participants; this question has been studied by many specialists, who maintain that such coherence is, precisely, one of the most valuable contributions of the concept of peacebuilding.

Bearing these ambiguities in mind, peacebuilding may be defined as a concerted effort involving the parties to a conflict in a given country, the UN, and representatives of the international community to develop lasting political, economic and social infrastructures in that country. Such coordination is conducive to reconciliation and reconstruction, while creating the conditions to prevent the resumption of armed conflict as a means of settling disputes.

Reconciliation and reconstruction are keywords in the strategy of peacebuilding. Their aim is to prevent the re-emergence of conditions that give rise to armed conflict. The merit of peacebuilding thus hinges on its capacity to change a potential or actual strife-ridden situation to a state of durable peace. The success of reconciliation and reconstruction relies on three series of objectives and missions, which cut across the different philosophies of peacebuilding.[9] These objectives are all the more critical in view of the fact that they come into play during a delicate period of transition when the outcome, be it peace or violence, is uncertain.

Security Transition

One of the primary objectives of peacebuilding is to prevent the resumption of violence. This entails the following tasks: disarming and demobilising combatants, re-integrating them into civilian life, reforming the armed forces and the police force, facilitating the safe return of refugees and displaced persons, de-mining areas affected by conflict and recovering light weapons. These tasks are shouldered in part by the UN peacekeeping forces, but they also involve civilian actors. During a period of security transition, the task of peacebuilding is not only to bring the conflict to an end (this is the mission of peacemaking), but also to monitor a truce or cease-fire (peacekeeping), and to impose a truce (which would constitute peace enforcement). Peacebuilding, rather, contributes to eradicating the roots of a conflict, in the absence of violence.

Democratic Transition

The more political objectives involve creating conditions that are conducive to a process of democratisation. This means the participation of citizens in all levels of government, primarily through free elections that are closely monitored so as to guarantee their legitimacy and success. Democratisation also requires creating an environment in which human rights are respected, often in situations where they have long been violated. The administration of justice and penal reform (as well as the prosecution of criminals) are also elements of peacebuilding. However, this does not mean initiating mediation or negotiations between adversaries if such initiatives lie outside the existing constitutional framework (this would be conflict resolution).

Socio-economic Transition

The social and economic objectives of peacebuilding include rebuilding a society, a financial system and a government which are ill able to deliver basic services (drinking water, food, health, transportation, energy, etc.). In this case, the task is one of veritable reconstruction, often accompanied by a process of restructuring to promote economic recovery and enable the economy to generate the capital needed for rehabilitation. While reconstruction is a matter of urgency, the restructuring dimension of peacebuilding is linked to international development aid programs. It is not, however, a matter of solving the problems of under-development that may be partially, but not entirely, responsible for the flare-up of armed conflict. It can only be hoped that economic restructuring will help prevent a resurgence of violence.

What is the logic behind these missions? What philosophy underlies their efforts to change a situation of armed conflict?

THE THEORY OF PEACEBUILDING

In a recently published article, Roland Paris of Yale University correctly notes that the theoretical premises of the concept of peacebuilding have received little attention, while there is an abundance of accounts of peacebuilding missions (Paris, 1997, p. 55). This observation reflects a widespread impression that the motivation behind peacebuilding can only be neutral, since it stems from such good intentions: preventing violence, rebuilding, restructuring, disarmament and democratisation. But as Eva Bertram points out, 'At root, full-scale peacebuilding efforts are nothing short of attempts at nation building; they seek to remake a state's political institutions, security forces, and economic arrangements' (Bertram, 1995, pp. 38-39). Such reshaping is based on the export and application of a liberal approach to issues of security and democracy. The premises of this approach merit close examination, for the actual practice of peacebuilding may call their validity into question.

The Liberal Roots of Peacebuilding

Liberalism still represents, along with realism, one of the most influential currents of thought in international relations. Since the end of the Cold War, the expansion of the concept of security to include non-military aspects and the 'democratic triumph' of the West[10] have given liberalism renewed vitality. As a doctrine, it is rooted in the belief that the State exists to guarantee individual liberties and to democratically serve rather than dominate the collective will (as realism claims). Three ideas are central to the application of liberalism in the conduct of international relations:[11]

1) The appeal of values such as democracy is a force for peace among States and communities. In the Kantian view, the elements of a republican constitution (respect for individual freedoms, separation of powers, representative government, the rule of law) considerably reduce the belligerence of States. The modern thesis of 'democratic peace', according to which democratic States do not wage war against each another, stems from this idea.[12] As democracy spreads, so too do the chances for peace. As we shall see, this thesis is central

to the application of the concept of peacebuilding, particularly in the face of the problems raised by the issue of democratic transition.

2) Interdependence, particularly in the economic field, is also a force for peace to the extent that States (and communities) have more to lose than to gain by investing their resources in strategies of war. The theories of the classic author Sir Norman Angell rest on the belief that the surest road to peace is capitalism and especially free trade, which promises amicable relations among the nations.[13] According to liberals, the restructuring of a country according to free-market precepts is the best guarantee of integration into the world economy, prosperity, and hence stability. This thesis is also central to peacebuilding, since it supplies a justification for the efforts to carry out socio-economic conversion made by most peacebuilding missions.

3) Finally, international institutions can profitably take over from States in order to advance the liberal ideal, given their capacity to induce change in the behaviour of States through the use of the resources and prestige which international cooperation provides. In the area of security, classical institutionalists (such as David Mitrany and Ernst Haas) and neo-liberal institutionalists (such as John Ruggie and Robert Keohane) favour strengthening the role of international organisations as mediators.[14] Peacebuilding acts on this approach by giving these organisations a larger, central role in the security transition in States that are in the throes of a crisis or on the brink of dismemberment.

These three ideas converge to form a foundation for peacebuilding built on liberal principles and the Western tradition. If States in crisis, rising from the ashes of conflict, would take the democratic road (in other words, if they proceed with elections), move towards a market economy (that is, quickly adopt capitalism), and commit themselves to the solutions put forward by international institutions (primarily the UN, NATO, the IMF, the World Bank and NGOs), peace would surely be at hand. As Roland Paris has noted 'A single paradigm—liberal internationalism—appears to guide the work of most international agencies engaged in peacebuilding. The central tenet of this paradigm is the assumption that the surest foundation for peace, both within and between states, is market democracy, that is, a liberal democratic polity and a market-oriented economy' (Paris, 1997, p. 56).[15] It would thus suffice to export the market democracy model in order to secure a peace built on the basis of democratic and economic liberalism. Are such hopes well founded?

Peacebuilding to the Rescue of the Liberal Agenda

Peacebuilding constitutes a response to new security problems which have emerged since the end of the Cold War, and the liberal approach which we have described claims to possess the necessary tools for promoting peace under these new conditions. As Stanley Hoffmann, one of the proponents of this approach, puts it, 'there is another enemy in today's world: not the violence that results from the clash of mighty powers or from the imposition of the power of the strong on the weak, but the violence that results from chaos from below. The world today is threatened by the disintegration of power -- by anomie, which denotes the absence of norms' (Hoffmann, 1995, p. 167).[16] In the minds of many of these theorists, peacebuilding is, implicitly, one of the ways in which anomie could be addressed and security therefore strengthened through international adhesion to liberal standards of peace (Stremlau, 1995, pp. 397-412).[17] These standards rest on a foundation that embraces three security components:

1) *A 'positive', rather than 'negative', conception of peace.*[18] While peace is negatively defined by the absence of organised violence between communities and nations, a positive definition focuses on the absence of structural violence, defined as the development of factors of cooperation and integration between communities and nations in order to promote lasting peace. While the Cold War made it impossible to go much beyond 'negative' peace (indeed, it thrived on it as a strategy), in the past ten years this approach has been considered unsuitable for containing conflict and addressing the anomie of the international system. Hence the interest in promoting peace by acting on political, socio-economic and security factors with the aim of eliminating violence. Transition strategies of peacebuilding largely espouse the 'positive peace'

approach.

2) *Emphasising the notion of 'human security.'*[19] It is by no means surprising that among the countries most favourable to peacebuilding are those that advocate a novel view of security. For example, a liberal country like Canada is defending the new idea of 'human security', which means 'security against economic privation, an acceptable quality of life, and a guarantee of fundamental human rights'. The notion supposes 'at a minimum that basic needs are met, but it also acknowledges that sustained economic development, human rights and fundamental freedoms, the rule of law, good governance, sustainable development and social equity are as important to global peace as arms control and disarmament' (Minister Axworthy, 1996, pp. 1-2). Canada thus sees peacebuilding as the 'keystone' of human security.

3) *The use of 'cooperative security' mechanisms.*[20] This approach has highlighted the benefits of multilateral cooperation in order to solve problems of joint security in a spirit of partnership, particularly since the end of the Cold War. It operates primarily through multilateral mechanisms and international organisations. Peacebuilding relies, first and foremost, on the cooperative security approach, since its demands for resources can mostly be marshalled through multilateral aid.

'Positive peace', 'human security' and 'cooperative security' constitute standards that are meant to further the agenda of peacebuilding and the interests of a stable liberal order within the international system. These standards now shape, in whole or in part, the conduct of certain forms of foreign policy—to the point where they are seen as a 'new interventionism' (Stedman, 1993, pp. 1-16) or as 'social work' (Mandelbaum, 1996, pp. 16-32) (in the case of the US), or as the vocation of a 'middle power' (C.P. David & D. Bourgeois, 1997) (in the case of Canada). Can peacebuilding really come to the rescue of liberalism and vindicate the foreign policies that support it and apply it? Hopes must be tempered by caution: prudence is warranted in applying these standards.

THE PRACTICE OF PEACEBUILDING

'Does peacebuilding build peace?' also asks Roland Paris. He answers the question in the negative on the basis of eight case studies of peacebuilding.[21] The studies reveal a wide gap between expectations and the outcome of the efforts invested in peacebuilding. According to Paris, transplanting the liberal model of market democracy encounters unforeseen obstacles at best, and at worst engenders perverse effects to the point of jeopardising the peace it assumes has been achieved. He argues that the very nature of political and economic transition (we might add security transition) is responsible for the unintended consequences. Political stability and economic prosperity depend on competition, albeit regulated, which all save one of the countries studied could not sustain. This, in spite of the fact that the countries in question underwent a process of democratisation, adopted a market economy, and followed the advice of international organisations and agencies. The problem lay with factors beyond the control of these countries, in particular the fact that the standards that peacebuilding calls for often collide with prevailing local conditions.

Liberalisation that is too fast-paced appears to exacerbate rather than resolve the problem of violence. The danger thus lies in the possibility that peace may ultimately be rendered more fragile rather than strengthened. The reasons for this disappointing outcome may reside in the way in which the delicate processes of security, democratic and socio-economic transitions are carried out. Arguably, it is not sufficient to export and apply the liberal model of peacebuilding in order to secure a lasting peace.

Security Transition

It is not an easy matter to conclude a peace agreement, and it is even more difficult to consolidate that peace. Certain security situations readily lend themselves to the practice of conflict resolution (such was the case for example in Namibia, El Salvador and Nicaragua), because of the sustained commitment and considerable influence of third parties involved in the process.[22] Other cases, by contrast, have not yielded equally positive outcomes, despite equally sustained outside intervention (Angola, Bosnia, Cambodia and Somalia, among others). Why does the security transition sometimes jeopardise peacebuilding? Why does peacebuilding sometimes aggravate that transition? These are sensitive questions, which have received little attention.

Security transition must take into account certain realities that may diminish the chances of success of peacebuilding efforts. In particular, three elements of 'realist' analysis need to be considered: the balance of forces in the wake of a civil war, the effect of the security dilemma on the former combatants, and control over the territory.

1) *The balance of forces in the wake of a civil war.* The negotiated end of a conflict has real consequences for the forces in the field. Certain structural elements of the conflict, which may vary considerably from one war situation to the other, influence the course of events once hostilities cease and the difficult process of reconciliation begins. According to Charles King, understanding the factors which prompt violence, from the vantage point of the belligerents, leads to a rather discouraging conclusion: the more closely an internal conflict resembles a civil war (for example, Angola, Cambodia, Bosnia), the more resistant it is to a peaceful settlement (King, 1993). Unless peace is externally enforced (Bosnia), peace accords either prove to be precarious (Cambodia) or lead to greater instability (Angola).

Analysing post-civil war situations, King demonstrates that in the majority of cases where there is no strong peace enforcement by third parties (Fen Hampson's thesis), negotiated peace accords result in more unstable outcomes than when one of the parties to the conflict won on the battlefield. All peacebuilding operations, observes King, 'except Namibia, Nicaragua and El Salvador resulted in the defection of a signatory to the agreement and the resumption of violence' (King, 1997, p. 58).

The main reason for this impasse is attributed to 'spoilers', who resort to deceit in order to win on the battlefield what they could not get at the negotiating table. Such deceit obstructs all peacebuilding strategies that rely on disarmament and demobilisation (Angola is a good example of such a situation). In a similar vein, John Stedman maintains that only sustained political and military involvement, backed up by a threat of intervention, can restrain the 'spoilers'. Otherwise, the situation may quickly deteriorate -- depending on the type of 'spoiler' involved -- to the point of dashing hopes for any stable peace. According to Stedman, 'such parties [spoilers] can only be defeated; they cannot be appeased through negotiation' (Stedman, 1995, p. 56). In Cambodia and Angola, it was the absence of peace (re) enforcement that largely undermined the international efforts to implement agreements that had been duly negotiated and applied (Stedman, 1995, pp. 5-53).

A realistic strategy for peacebuilding must take into account the fact that the balance of forces may have a greater bearing on the chances for a peaceful security transition than does a negotiated agreement. The prognosis is not encouraging, unless there is external intervention to preserve the existing state of affairs and prevent any change in the balance of forces. 'While external powers today work assiduously to encourage belligerents to settle their differences at the negotiating table rather than on the battlefield', notes King, 'such attempts run against the tide of history' (King, 1997, p. 25). Frequently, backing for external intervention is also based on the assumption that the security dimension of peacebuilding can be handled with relative 'neutrality' or 'impartiality'. The experience in Somalia (Clarke and Herbot, 1996, pp. 70-85) and Bosnia (Betts, 1994, pp. 20-33), where 'conflicts must be intensified before they are resolved' (Stedman, 1995, p. 20),[23] clearly demonstrates the fallacy of this approach -- a conclusion which is at variance, to say the least, with the cause of peacebuilding.

2) *The effects of the 'security dilemma' on ex-combatants.*[24] The lack of trust among combatants is one of the central problems of the security transition. In this sense, it introduces uncertainty into the process of implementing the accords, since the preferences of the parties to the conflict, and the compromises they are prepared to make, are never clear.[25] The structural elements of a conflict intensify in several ways the security dilemma, wherein the protagonists see their own survival as decidedly more important than implementation of the peace agreement.[26]

First, the values and identities of the parties to a civil war are often so incompatible that, in spite of the best of intentions, it may be impossible to prevent a resumption of hostilities, for the parties cannot imagine themselves living in a state of peaceful coexistence. Victory for one and defeat for the other become the objective in a situation where the peace was already fragile. Under such conditions, agreements on disarmament, the recovery of weapons and de-mining may have no impact on the security dilemma in the long run, if the combatants still want to fight (A good illustration of this logic is the activities of factions that are fearful of, or hostile to, peace in Cambodia and Angola).

Secondly, the attitude of leaders is a determining factor to the extent that they have interests to defend, political and military clients to satisfy (both internal and external to the conflict) and the will to win on the ground (whether by constitutional means or not). The treatment reserved for the leaders of factions that participated in the violence is, incidentally, a sensitive aspect of peacebuilding: should peace be built with them or should they be prosecuted? Peacebuilding can sometimes mean dealing with leaders who are diametrically opposed to the liberal ideal. The resolution of the security dilemma can involve compromises that ultimately result in the pursuit of peacebuilding on a basis that is contrary to the principle of equitable security.

Finally, the problem of making and carrying out decisions in the delicate context of a peacebuilding mission should not be underestimated. The situation can deteriorate to the point of jeopardising the agreements reached among the warring factions. Internal divisions within the belligerents (between 'hawks' and 'doves'), material incentives (war booty), a culture of violence (that confounds any hope for disarmament), the pressures of partisans or opponents of peace are all potent factors that generate risks of heightened tension and reduce the possibility of convergence of objectives among these groups. Securing the battlefield to promote non-violent resolution of political conflicts can be quite difficult under such circumstances (combatants may hold forces in reserve in order to ensure their survival in the event of a worsening of the security dilemma). An apparently stable peace, which is in reality temporary, can thus permit belligerent 'spoilers' to retrench and fight again another day.

3) *Control over territory*. In a period of peacebuilding, security transition means the ability to demobilise combatants, repatriate refugees and build a national police force to ensure public order and safety in a devastated State. In situations other than civil war, such objectives can be achieved with reasonable hope for success (Namibia and Haiti, for example). In the context of a civil war, control over territory is a subject of conflict and the division of territory is the objective of the (former) combatants. Seldom is this objective relinquished, even though the signed and consolidated peace settlement provides for a supposedly indivisible territory. This is probably the reason for the resumption of violence within five years after the signing of a peace agreement in 50 percent of cases (Licklider, 1995, p. 686). A realistic solution that remains largely unacceptable within a peacebuilding perspective would consist of separating the warring parties and dividing the territory. In certain cases (and Bosnia could very well become one) partition is the only means to ensure a genuine security transition and a lasting peace (Mearsheimer, 1997, A-13). [27]

Having studied this issue, Chaim Kaufmann concludes: 'the data supports the argument that separation of groups is the key to ending ethnic civil wars ... There is not a single case where non-ethnic civil politics were created or restored by reconstruction of ethnic identities, power-sharing coalitions, or state-building' (Kaufmann, 1996, p. 161). [28] The territorial partition that Kaufmann endorses is in direct contradiction with the liberal precepts of peacebuilding. Kaufmann argues that, in order to save lives and avoid genocide, the danger of which is ever present, external interventions should not attempt the reconstruction of multiethnic States (unless imposed by force). They should instead facilitate and protect the movement of the population to distinct territories. According to Kaufmann's line of reasoning, the security dilemma would be reduced if, rather than favouring territorial integrity, outside powers accepted the idea of territorial division. 'In ethnic wars', contends Kaufmann, 'saving lives may require ignoring state-centered legal norms' (Kaufmann, 1996, p. 161). This provocative thesis occasionally finds supporting evidence in cases such as Bosnia and Rwanda, where the efforts invested in peacebuilding, modest as they may have been, have failed to guarantee ideal conditions for a successful security transition.

The gulf separating the negotiating table from the battlefield appears to remain as wide in the wake of a conflict as it was during its active prosecution, making peacebuilding an extremely complex operation when it comes to security -- and certainly not as easy as suggested by the theorists of the concept. In order to succeed and overcome the legacy of a civil war, peacebuilding requires a strong dose of enforcement.

Democratic Transition

In the minds of most of the people involved in peacebuilding operations, peacebuilding comes down to 'organising elections'.[29] Similarly, proponents of 'democratic peace' often, and wrongly, establish an equation between democracy and peace.[30] Ultimately, the political dimension of the transition raises excessive hopes for ending the conflict. Achieving political pluralism is not, however, a simple task. All the peacebuilding operations conducted since 1989 have been based on a promise of democratisation and elections under UN auspices. At least half of them, in the view of many observers, have ended in failure: Cambodia, Angola, Rwanda and particularly, Bosnia.[31]

While the 1989 elections brought the peace process in Namibia to a successful conclusion (in the absence of a civil war), the 1993 elections in Cambodia had the opposite effect: they exacerbated political divisions between the parties and set the stage for the violent confrontations of 1997 which shook the fragile constitutional edifice put in place by the UN. In Angola, the 1992 elections did not succeed in bringing about reconciliation between the former enemies. Refusing to accept its electoral defeat, UNITA picked up its weapons again in an attempt to reverse its political losses on the battlefield. In El Salvador, the 1994 elections have not solved, for the time being, the problem of 'death squads', which react vengefully to the inclusion of the former FMLN rebels in the political process as a recognised opposition party. In Rwanda, the planned 1995 elections heightened fears within the dominant Hutu faction of an impending electoral defeat, precipitating one of the most horrific genocide in history. Finally, in Bosnia, the 1996 elections were, to be sure, carried out in an orderly fashion (under the watchful eye of NATO peacekeeping troops), but they enshrined ethnic divisions instead of closing them. In short, the process of democratisation did not live up to expectations. Why?

1) *Democratic competition.* Democratic competition is both common and healthy in countries with a long-established tradition of civic participation. The practice is, however, alien to countries with no democratic tradition.[32] Democracy means accepting political competition as the way to contest and win, by legitimate means, the status of government representing the majority of the people. While political conflict is normal within established democracies, it is difficult to manage in countries where democratic institutions need to be built from scratch. Under these conditions, 'encouraging political activity can polarise the populace into a number of separated, potentially hostile communities' (Paris, 1997, p. 75). Maintaining civic spirit becomes difficult, and elections (the main standard used to judge the political outcome of peacebuilding) turn out to be a risky venture.

Instead of strengthening the process of democratisation, political competition becomes, in certain cases, a destabilising factor which can re-ignite violent conflict. Democracy, as Roland Paris reminds us, is not the cause of violence as such. Rather, it is the political competition that sustains democracy that often sharpens conflict instead of muting it in a deeply divided and fragile society (which was the case, he notes, in Angola, Rwanda and Bosnia). A number of Africa experts have underscored the importance of developing a democratic tradition, independently of socio-economic development, for the process of establishing peaceful relations. And on the basis of this criterion alone, they are quite pessimistic about prospects for democracy in Africa.[33]

Elections, even when supported by external powers, rarely settle the fundamental issue of political competition as a legitimate process, recognised and accepted by all. 'The experiences of countries as diverse as Angola or Cambodia', observes Krishna Kumar, 'unmistakably show that the ruling political parties seek to manipulate elections without compunction [free and fair elections] do not necessarily transform a society's deep-rooted political structures and culture' (Kumar, 1997, p. 8). In other words, the electoral process does not ultimately guarantee that political competition will become an institutionalised practice in the society in question.

2) *The redistribution of political power.* Democratisation within the context of a peacebuilding operation is not a neutral process. It entails a redistribution of power and competition for political control, which in a country devastated by war has an impact quite different than it does in countries free of violence. Political control is pursued by factions that gave up their weapons (sometimes temporarily) in order to compete in the political arena. The transition period between the state of violence and democracy represents, in this sense, a twilight zone. There is no guarantee that parties recently locked in conflict will give free rein to democratic institutions and be respectful of them. Each practices the politics of scapegoating, blaming the opponent for the failures of democracy in order to seize power and reverse the process of democratisation.[34] The period of redistribution of power is thus characterised by instability. Each party weighs its chances of gaining or losing in this redistribution. It is hardly surprising to note, according to the analysis of Edward Mansfield and Jack Snyder, that '*democratising* states -- those that have recently undergone regime change in a democratic direction -- are much more war-prone than states that have undergone no regime change' (Mansfield and Snyder, 1995, p. 8).[35]

The challenge, warns Winrich Kühne, resides in 'remov[ing] all political reasons to use weapons' (Kühne, 1996, xxv). This done, the redistribution of power could make it more advantageous either to accept the authority of the stronger faction, or adopt a form of power sharing between the major rival factions in order to preserve stability. In either case, this realistic choice would undermine the prospects for democracy. This choice gives absolute priority to peace over democracy. It assumes that, contrary to the thesis of 'democratic peace', it is peace that brings democracy and not the reverse. The issue here is of crucial importance given the emphasis peacebuilding issue here is of crucial importance given the emphasis peacebuilding missions place on organising elections.

Paradoxically, to proceed precipitously with elections may turn out to be the least productive way to build peace and ensure the emergence of democracy. On this point, the 1996 Berlin conference arrived at the following conclusion: 'The UN is putting too much emphasis on elections. Elections within a fragmented society lead to further fragmentation. What is required are models of power-sharing, like governments of national unity. Western style democracy will not work in developing countries' (Kühne, 1996, p. 92). Hasty elections are not, therefore, a panacea. They are often extremely costly when they are the continuation of war by other means. Rather than sharing power, one or more of the opposing factions can simply ignore or, in extreme cases, militarily contest the results.[36] In the first case, the electoral process contributes nothing to the democratic transition; in the second, it weakens it.

3) *The problem of 'illiberal democracies'*. This expression is used by Fareed Zakaria to indicate that elections are not the sole criterion for the existence of democracy. On the contrary, he maintains, we are witnessing a proliferation of false democracies (which he calls 'illiberal democracies') that show little or no respect for the real foundations of constitutional liberalism, notably the rule of law and individual freedoms. According to Zakaria 'Constitutional liberalism has led to democracy, but democracy does not seem to bring constitutional liberalism.' And, he adds, without liberalism, 'the introduction of democracy in divided societies has actually fomented nationalism, ethnic conflict, and even war' (Zakaria, 1997, pp. 28, 35).[37] On this view, it is not democracy but constitutional liberalism that sows the seeds of peace. Zakaria's analysis echoes and refines the Kantian view, valuing the benefits of liberal peace over democratic peace. What peacebuilding missions must promote, then, is not elections but rather a process of conversion to and education in constitutional liberalism. The author concludes that more imaginative approaches to constitutional transition must be sought (which is not necessarily encouraging from a Canadian perspective).

Socio-economic Transition

Peacebuilding aims to quickly convert the countries targeted for rehabilitation to capitalism. Like the recipe for democracy, the economic solutions of reconstruction and restructuring are supposed to bring about the stability required for lasting peace. Without entering into a general discussion of the relationship between the economy, development and security (for this see, among others, Jean-François Rioux and Robin Hay[38]), it is important to examine the unforeseen effects of peacebuilding on two specific facets of the socio-economic transition.

Reconstruction is the least problematic task in the process, despite the magnitude of the need. In countries that have been torn by strife, the people often welcome offers of assistance to carry out various urgent tasks: restoring social services (health, education, nutrition), helping war victims, particularly women and children, and repairing infrastructures to enable the administration and distribution of essential services. In many countries, peacebuilding missions have responded effectively and satisfactorily to these needs. According to Krishna Kumar, 'In fact, the international community seems to have been more effective in social rehabilitation than in political reconstruction partly because of its relatively long involvement in social sectors, such as health and education. Non-governmental organisations, in particular, have played a critical role in rebuilding these sectors' (Kumar, 1997, p. 15). At the same time, some national and international initiatives are helping to increase the civilian resources available for rebuilding tasks. The Argentinean project that led to the creation of the UN White Helmets volunteer corps in 1995 is an example.[39]

On the other hand, the restructuring dimension raises many problems. For many countries, externally planned economic transition is painful. The restructuring demanded by institutions such as the IMF and the World Bank in order to ensure long-term stability generally has nefarious effects on the process of peacebuilding (Paris, 1997, pp. 66-70). For example, the austerity measures imposed on El Salvador have substantially diminished the resources available for integrating former fighters into civilian life. The result has been an increase in criminal violence against a backdrop of economic recession. Considered appropriate from the standpoint of economic liberalism, these measures are of little help from the perspective of peacebuilding. Nicaragua is also in the grips of a similar dilemma. The restructuring process is pursuing the objective of developing a market economy at the cost of a serious deterioration in living standards, resulting in pauperisation and a concomitant resurgence of violence. Finally, the process of economic liberalisation in Mozambique is undermining government efforts to rehabilitate the population and restore infrastructures, leading to widespread banditry in rural areas. What then do these cases show about the potentially harmful impact of restructuring on peace?

1) *Economic competition and its social consequences.* Like democracy, capitalism is founded on competition between producers within a free market. However, such competition engenders inequalities in the accumulation and distribution of wealth. Beyond a certain point, these inequalities can foster discontent, misery and confrontation, particularly in societies that are poor and tested by violence. An excessively rapid and harsh process of economic liberalisation ('shock therapy') increases inequalities and heightens social tensions. Under such conditions, the 'magic' of the free market can be quite difficult to export to countries where peacebuilding efforts are underway (just as it was found in the 1960s that modernisation theories proved futile when applied to the Third World). As a result, says Roland Paris, restructuring efforts 'tend to make war-shattered states more fragile and vulnerable to the destabilising effects of economic and political liberalisation than other states at similar levels of economic or political development' (Paris, 1997, p. 78). Moreover, in El Salvador and Nicaragua as in Mozambique, some factions would like to continue reaping the profits of violent activities (such as arms trafficking), which can only aggravate the difficulty of converting previously war-based economies to productive civilian activities.

As a consequence, not only democratic reform but also capitalist reform could prove less than optimal for peacebuilding. Furthermore, risks are often greater when these two types of restructuring are conducted simultaneously. This is borne out, according to *The*

Economist, by the African experience: 68 structural reform programs guided by the IMF in 36 poor countries resulted in rising political and social unrest, to the point of threatening the viability of the reforms. *The British Weekly* concludes: 'The original idea that economic reform and democracy would together bring political stability and economic prosperity has not yet been vindicated' (*The Economist*, September 20, 1997, p. 49).

2) *Dependence versus development*. Short-term humanitarian and financial assistance is vital to the survival of a country. It can, however, become unproductive for peacebuilding in the long term. As Winrich Kühne notes, 'Relief programmes have a strong tendency to create and sustain dependencies. This is a cardinal issue impacting negatively on self-reliance and development...On occasion, assistance may even be counterproductive, aggravating the political relationship between the parties in dispute' (Kühne, 1996, p. 75). There is, in this sense, a certain contradiction between UN and NGO peace missions on one hand and the state of economic marginalisation of poor countries on the other. As the number of such missions increases, the process of marginalisation intensifies, according to Timothy Shaw: stagnant or declining economic performance, antagonistic social classes, a widening gap between rich and poor, declining educational, health and infra structural standards, and rising levels of private violence (Shaw, 1996, p. 41).[40]
If democratisation and capitalism, supported by development projects, cannot always guarantee stability in countries which have been spared the ravages of war, we may well question the ability of the political and economic liberalism that drives peacebuilding to produce stability in countries that have been torn apart by strife.

3) *Lack of consistency between security and financial interventions*. Lack of coherence between the UN (primarily) on one hand and the IMF and the World Bank on the other is one of the weak links in the socio-economic transition which peacebuilding seeks to achieve. Many participants in UN operations point to the damage done by the incompatibility in objectives. Suzan Willett describes the current conflict in Mozambique, where the UN's priority is human security and the IMF is prioritising economic restructuring. Willett sees the conflict as a reflection of the

contradiction between two antagonistic visions, which are generating needless misery and violence (Willett, 1995, p. 44). Alvaro de Soto and Graciana del Castillo analyse the case of El Salvador, which they consider to be a fine illustration of the lack of coordination between different UN agencies. The authors compare the peace process and restructuring plans to 'children of different families', and El Salvador to 'a patient lay[ing] on the operating table with the left and right sides of his body separated by a curtain and unrelated surgery being performed on each side' (de Soto and del Castillo, 1994, pp. 72, 74). The result for the country is a situation in which the security transition and socio-economic transition are being carried out each to the detriment of the other. This lack of coordination could eventually jeopardise the still-fragile peace that has been negotiated in El Salvador. Peacebuilding carries with it unforeseen risks. It also presents choices that turn out to be more problematic than could have been foreseen from the liberal blueprint.

CONCLUSION

While the concept of peacebuilding has its limitations and must overcome certain obstacles that we have attempted to identify, the obstacles to its application do not mean that all hope for reconciliation and reconstruction in war-torn countries must be abandoned. A total withdrawal of these missions would constitute an unacceptable admission of impotence on the part of the UN, its member states and the NGOs. Moreover, it would result in a more fragmented and chaotic world. Expanding operations in order to export the liberal model of market democracy on a still wider scale would be equally perilous in the absence of more rigorous analysis of the model's impact on the development of recipient countries.

Some experts cited above, such as Roland Paris, suggest that we scale down our expectations of peacebuilding and act with circumspection: the process of democratisation must be controlled and gradual, even if this means postponing premature elections; the economic philosophy of 'shock therapy', which increases the risk of mass impoverishment and civil strife, must be reconsidered; civilian and military activities must be more effectively coordinated in order to avoid excessive confusion and decentralisation; and more realistic timeframes, up to nine years perhaps, should be set for peacebuilding missions. [41]

These recommendations warrant more thorough examination, based on a larger number of cases, in order to better assess the long-term viability of the concept of peacebuilding. More detailed studies would also help avoid the deployment of resources and manpower where peace, viewed from a realistic perspective, may prove difficult to consolidate. As Boutros-Ghali has himself noted, 'peacebuilding is not a therapy that the United Nations can attempt to impose on an unwilling patient' (Boutros-Ghali, 1996, p. 317).

APPENDIX

Evaluation Criteria for Peacebuilding Missions

In light of this conceptual and empirical survey, and in order to facilitate the evaluation of case studies of peacebuilding, we propose the following criteria and questions as an analytic guide:[42]

1) *The Nature of the Mission*

a) Does the operation match the 'exclusivist' or 'inclusivist' definition of peacebuilding? What role does it assign to development as opposed to the more short-term process of reconstruction?

b) At what stage of the peace process is the mission being conducted? Is the mission based on a 'gradualist' or a 'synergist' approach?

c) To what extent is the consent of the parties indispensable to the mission's success?

d) Which actors (States, international, military, civilian organisations) are involved in the conduct of the mission? How coherent are the mission's decision-making and operational processes?

2) *Security Transition*
    a) Is the balance of forces that has emerged from the conflict stable, or is it threatened by 'spoilers'? Does it enhance or diminish the chances for a peaceful transition? Should peace be externally enforced, and what would be the consequences for the process of building peace?
    b) How is the security dilemma affecting the combatants? What are the attitudes of the different factions, and how do they make the prospects for peacebuilding more or less realistic?
    c) Is control over the territory a major issue (with violent implications), and if so, is the mission capable of overcoming the obstacles to safeguarding the territorial integrity of the State?

3) *Democratic Transition*
    a) Is the democratisation process, and particularly the holding of elections, bringing the hoped-for political stability, or is it contributing to the re-emergence of violence between the parties?
    b) What impact is the transition having on the redistribution of political power? Is it sufficiently satisfactory to the parties so as to prevent the resumption of violence?
    c) Is the democratisation process succeeding in establishing a liberal constitutional framework that can be accepted and respected by all parties to the conflict?

4) *Socio-economic Transition*
    a) What are the social consequences of economic (and particularly financial) restructuring programs? Are these consequences fostering political tensions that could imperil the cause of peacebuilding?
    b) Is dependence on aid and reconstruction programs improving the prospects for development, or is it aggravating conditions of economic marginalisation?
    c) Is there coherence among the participants in the mission in regard to its security and financial aspects? What are the effects of incoherence, if any, on the process of socio-economic transition?

NOTES

A short version of this chapter appeared in *Security Dialogue*, vol. 30, no. 1 (1999). The author appreciates the journal for clearing copyrights.

1. The mission ended in 1998, when the UN left Eastern Slovenia and transferred responsibility to Croatia for the administration of territories that it had administered for two years.

2. NATO's stabilisation missions (SFOR) and the missions to rebuild the police force and the civil affairs bureau conducted by the United Nations in Bosnia-Herzegovina (UNMBH).

3. A survey of the UN missions in the last ten years is presented in Fetherston (1994) and S. Han (1994).

4. An analysis of the new conditions, which are more conducive to the application of the concept of peacebuilding, is presented by C. P. David, et al. (1997).

5. See report on the Berlin conference edited by W. Kühne (1996).

6. This is what could be inferred from B. Boutros-Ghali *op. cit.*, p. 22 (reference to 1995 text) as well as B. Boutros-Ghali (1994) pp. 5-6; the developmental perspective on peacebuilding is studied by Jean-François Rioux and Robin Hay (1997); by Kenneth Bush (1995); and by Necla Tschirgi (February 7, 1997).

7. Distinctions between these concepts are explained in UN Department of Public Information (1990, pp. 3-9); William Durch, ed., (1996, pp. 1-34); Thomas Milburn (March-April 1997, pp. 3-9); Denis McLean (1996, pp. 1-4); A. B. Fethertston (1994, pp. 125-131); and Michael Lund (1997, pp. 399-400).

8. B. Boutros-Ghali reasserts: 'the primary condition for the engagement of the United Nations in post-conflict peacebuilding must be consent of the parties concerned', in Winrich Kühne, p. x.

E. Bertram adds that at a minimum the government exercising power must give its consent, (Bertram, 1995, p. 388).

9. For the missions and objectives of peacebuilding, see Department for Economic and Social Information and Policy Analysis (1996, p. 62); K. Kumar (1997); N. Ball (1996); J. Chopra (1997, pp. 177-189); J. King (1997, pp. 20-26); E. Bertram (1995, pp. 388-400); S. Han (1995, pp. 871-875).

10. The triumph of liberalism, which is inspiring new confidence in the possibility of lasting peace, has been forcefully propounded by Francis Fukuyama (1992). This triumph has been called into question by the equally controversial thesis of Samuel Huntington (1996).

11. An overview of the liberal approach is given by T. Dunne (1997) and by D. Baldwin (ed.) (1993).

12. There is a large body of literature on the subject. One of the best syntheses of the theory of democratic peace is presented by S. Chan (1997).

13. The thesis of peace through trade and interdependence is explored in C.P. David and A. Benessaieh (1997, pp. 227-254).

14. The field of security is rife with 'institutionalist liberals'. A concise introduction is provided by R. Keohane and L. Martin (1995, pp. 39-51). See the excellent review by M. Barnett (1997); also C. Kegley (ed.) (1995).

15. According to William Robinson's Gramscian analysis, liberal internationalism takes the form of 'polyarchic' hegemony (that is, decisions are made by small competing elites) which legitimise the American economic agenda (1996, pp. 457).

16. Many share Hoffmann's views on the advent of a 'dark age' in international relations as a result of the disintegration of the Westphalian system and the absence of any consensus on

common standards. Please refer to D. Bratt (1997, pp. 173-176), L. Neack (1997), and D. Gibbs (1997). On the other hand, this point of view is not shared by K. J. Holsti (1997), who argues that the Westphalian system is stable and cannot collapse into the dreaded state of chaos. Also see the analysis by J. Bowen (1996), who rejects the thesis of the proliferation of ethnic conflicts. For Bowen, such conflicts are essentially stirred up and driven by political elites.

17. The antidote to anarchy has always been founded on the search for mechanisms whereby a 'civil' order could be built in international relations, a quest which is by no means new; see the classic work by H. Bull (1977).

18. This concept is derived from the peace research school, which holds that violence is not inherent (as the realist school claims) but rather contingent upon attitudes, conditioning and learning (the liberal school). The proponents of this approach include Johan Galtung, who in the early 1970s was the first to consider the contribution of peacebuilding to the development of 'positive peace'. See J. Galtung (1976) and also A.B. Fetherston (1994, pp. 91-102).

19. The 'human security' school traces its conceptual roots to the writings of John Burton, for whom the denial of basic human needs is the source of conflict. According to Burton, once these needs are satisfied, 'positive peace' can ensue (1990, vol. 1 and 2); the Commission of Global Governance (led by Shridath Ramphal) (1995) ascribes an important role to human security within the larger objective of 'global security'. Also see M. Renner (1997, pp. 115-31) and T. Weiss and C. Collins (1996, pp. 13-38).

20. J. G. Ruggie provides a summary of the essential elements of 'cooperative security' (1996).

21. These studies deal with the following cases: Namibia, Cambodia, El Salvador, Nicaragua, Mozambique, Angola, Rwanda, and

Bosnia. In Paris' view, the only positive outcome was Namibia.

22. For peacemaking, see F. O. Hampson (1996, pp. 3-25) and C. A. Crocker and F. O. Hampson (1996).

23. In the same vein, a report published in India by the International Centre for Peace Initiatives (1997) acknowledges that 'conflicts, *per se*, can be constructive to the extent that they are agents of change. In some ways conflicts are inherent to the process of social development, state formation, and nation-building'. M. Ignatieff (1997) draws a similar conclusion in his latest book.

24. Applied to ethnic conflicts, the notion of 'security dilemma' refers to a lack of trust among ethnic rivals, as a result of which each over-estimates the ill intentions of the other. See B. Posen (1993).

25. S. J. Stedman and D. Rothchild (1996) have studied this issue and recommend the adoption of 'security-building measures' to diminish the effect of false perceptions. These measures resemble the 'confidence-building measures' of the Cold War, but the authors acknowledge that their application in an entirely different theatre of operations requires a strong dose of realism.

26. This analysis is inspired by C. King (1997, pp. 29-53). Also see E. Bertram (1995, pp. 396-400 and pp. 405-406).

27. See also similar arguments by M. Glitman (1996-97), J. Shear (1996), and J.M.O. Sharp (1997-98).

28. This analysis is similar to S. Van Evera's discussion.

29. We are dealing here only with the electoral aspect of the democratic transition. It must be borne in mind that the judicial and penal dimensions are equally essential to accomplish this transition. See W. Kühne (1996, pp. 81-95) and K. Kumar (1997, pp. 9-11).

30. The equation should rather be made between the republican form

of government and perpetual peace, as elaborated in Kantian philosophy, that is, the pre-eminence of the rule of law and of the principle of individual liberty. Kant remained sceptical, however, about the rule of majority consent, and according to S. Chan (1997, p. 64), he would not have considered himself a 'democrat' if that rule is taken to mean respect for popular will.

31. See the empirical studies by J. Chopra (1996, pp. 335-357), R. Paris (1997, pp. 64-73), S. J. Stedman (1997, pp. 19-44), W. Kühne (1996, pp. 11-47), and S. Han (1994, pp. 843-867).

32. Even in Haiti, which is a successful example of peacebuilding, a culture of brutality persists and the recent elections have exacerbated political divisions. 'Haiti shows why outsiders should not count on rapidly changing a political culture deformed by centuries of dictatorship' (*The New York Times*, December 11, 1997, pp. A-12).

33. See, among others, Harbeson (1997).

34. Ethnic rivalries are a fertile ground for scapegoating. The case is convincingly argued by R. de Nevers (1993, pp. 31-48) and V. P. Gagnon (1994-95, pp. 331-367).

35. Mohammed Ayoub notes that in European history 'democracy emerged as the final stage of the state-building process' (and not the first), an observation which, in his view, is still more pertinent for the Third World. See C. Crocker and F. Hampson (1996).

36. On this subject, the study of N. Ball and T. Halevy (1996) is prescient.

37. The thesis is also supported by International Centre for Peace Initiatives (1997, pp. 60-70). A still more provocative (and questionable) thesis is argued by Robert Kaplan, already famous for his vision of 'coming anarchy'. For Kaplan, 'democratic peace' does not apply to developing countries (and still less to underdeveloped countries). In his view, these countries need (1)

still less to underdeveloped countries). In his view, these countries need (1) the growth of an economically prosperous middle class, and (2) a form of authoritarian government capable of preventing civil violence (along the Chinese rather than the Indian model). Kaplan maintains that 'democracy is a fraud in many poor countries...: Africans want a better life and instead have been given the right to vote' (1997, p. 80). However, the 'myth of authoritarianism' is critiqued in the collection of articles edited by L. Diamond and M. Plattner (1995, p. 252).

38. J. F. Rioux and R. Hay (1997) present an excellent analysis of this relationship.

39. Refer to C. P. David and F. J. Valiente (1997). See also the journal *White Helmets*, vol. 1, no. 1 (1997), published in Buenos Aires, which provides a comprehensive review of White Helmet activities and projects.

40. See also J. Ginifer (1996).

41. These suggestions are taken in large part from R. Paris (1997, pp. 79-89) who proposes that peacebuilding follow a more prudent 'strategic liberalisation' approach.

42. GRIPCI will conduct three case studies of peacebuilding. The selected countries are in a state of constant evolution and therefore merit particular attention. They are Guatemala, Haiti and Bosnia.

REFERENCES

D. Baldwin (ed.), *Neorealism and Neoliberalism: The Contemporary Debate* (New York: Columbia University Press, 1993).

N. Ball, 'The Challenge of Rebuilding War-Torn Societies' in C. Crocker, et al. (eds), *Managing Global Chaos. Sources and Responses to International Conflict* (Washington, D.C.: United States Institute of Peace Press, 1996).

N. Ball and T Halevy, *Making Peace Work: The Role of the International Development Community* (Washington, D.C.: Overseas Development Council, 1996).

M. Barnett, 'Bringing in the New World Order. Liberalism, Legitimacy, and the United Nations', *World Politics*, vol. 49 (July 1997), pp. 526-551.

E. Bertram, 'Reinventing Governments: The Promise and Perils of United Nations Peace-building', *Journal of Conflict Resolution*, vol. 39 (September 1995), pp. 387-418.

R. Betts, 'The Delusion of Impartial Intervention', *Foreign Affairs*, vol. 73 (November-December 1994), pp. 20-33.

J. Bowen, 'The Myth of Global Ethnic Conflict', *Journal of Democracy*, vol. 7 (October 1996), pp. 3-14.

D. Bratt, 'Rebuilding Fractured Societies', *Security Dialogue*, vol 28, no. 2 (June 1997), pp. 173-176.

H. Bull, *The Anarchical Society: A Study of Order in World Politics* (New York: Columbia University Press, 1977).

J. Burton, *Conflict: Resolution and Provention*, vol. 1 and *Conflict Human Needs Theory*, vol. 2 (London: MacMillan, 1990).

K. Bush, 'Towards a Balanced Approach to Rebuilding War-Torn Societies', *Canadian Foreign Policy,* vol. 3 (Winter 1995), pp 49-53.

Canadian Centre for Foreign Policy Development, *National Forum on Canada's International Relations Report* (Ottawa: DFAIT 1996).

S. Chan, 'In Search of Democratic Peace: Problems and Promise *Mershon International Studies Review*, vol. 41 (May 1997), pp 59-92.

J. Chopra, 'The Space of Peace-Maintenance', *Political Geography*, vol. 15, nos. 3/4 (1996), pp. 3335-3337.

J. Chopra, 'The Peace-Maintenance Response', *Security Dialogue*, vol. 28, no. 2 (1997), pp. 177-89.

W. Clarke and J. Herbst, 'Somalia and the Future of Humanitarian Intervention', *Foreign Affairs*, vol. 75 (March-April 1996), pp. 70-85.

J. Cockell, *Peacebuilding in Canadian Foreign Policy: Policy and Operational Observations* (Ottawa: DFAIT, 1997).

Commission of Global Governance, *Our Global Neighbourhood* (Oxford: Oxford University Press, 1995).

C. Crocker and F. Hampson, 'Making Peace Settlements Work', *Foreign Policy*, no. 104 (Fall 1996), pp. 54-71.

C. P. David and A. Benessaieh, 'Théories sur l'interdépendance et les nouveaux problémes de sécurité', *Études Internationales*, vol. 28 (June 1997), pp. 227-254.

C. P. David and M. Bourgeois, 'Le Canada et la consolidation de la paix. La formulation d'une nouvelle approche pour la politique étrangère canadienne' (December 1997).

C. P. David, et al., 'After the Blue Helmets Come the White Helmets', *Peacekeeping and International Relations*, vol. 26 (January-February 1997), pp. 3-7.

C. P. David and F.J. Valiente, 'The Argentinian Initiative of the White Helmets in the Field of Peacebuilding', paper presented at the joint meeting of the *International Studies Association* and the *Asociacion Mexicana de Estudios Internacionales*, Manzanillo (December 1997).

Department of Economic and Social Information and Policy Analysis, *An Inventory of Post-Conflict Peacebuilding Activities* (New York: United Nations, 1996), p. 62.

L. Diamond and M. Plattner, *Economic Reform and Democracy* (Baltimore: Johns Hopkins University Press, 1995).

W. Durch (ed.), *UN Peacekeeping, American Politics, and the UN Civil Wars of the 1990s* (New York: St. Martin's Press, 1996).

T. Dunne, 'Liberalism', in J. Baylis and S. Smith (eds), *The Globalisation of World Politics: An Introduction to International Relations* (Oxford: Oxford University Press, 1997), pp. 147-163.

A. Fetherston, *Towards a Theory of United Nations Peacekeeping* (New York: St. Martin's Press, 1994).

R. Fisher, 'The Potential for Peacebuilding: Forging a Bridge from Peacekeeping to Peacemaking', *Peace and Change*, no. 18 (1993).

F. Fukuyama, *The End of History and the Last Man* (London: Hamilton, 1992).

V. P. Gagnon, 'Ethnic Nationalism and International Conflict', *International Security*, vol. 19 (Winter 1994-95), pp. 331-367.

J. Galtung, 'Twenty-Five Years of Peace Research: Ten Challenges and Some Responses', *Journal of Peace Research*, vol. 22, no. 2 (1985), pp. 141-158.

J. Galtung, 'Approaches to Peace: Peacekeeping, Peacemaking and Peacebuilding', *Peace, War and Defense: Essays in Peace Research*, vol. 3 (Copenhagen: Christian Ejlers, 1976).

B. B. Ghali, *An Agenda for Development* (New York: United Nations, 1994).

B. B. Ghali, *An Agenda for Peace*, 2nd edn (New York: United Nations, 1995).

B. B. Ghali, *The 50th Anniversary Annual Report on the Work of the Organisation* (New York: The United Nations, 1996).

D. Gibbs, 'Is Peacekeeping a New Form of Imperialism?' presented at the annual meeting of the *International Studies Association* (Toronto, March 1997).

M. Giltman, 'US Policy in Bosnia: A Flawed Approach', *Survival,* vol. 38 (Winter 1996-97), pp. 66-83.

J. Ginifer, 'Development and the UN Peace Mission: A New Interface Required?' *International Peacekeeping,* vol. 3 (Summer 1996), pp. 3-13.

F. Hampson, *Nurturing Peace: Why Peace Settlements Succeed or Fail* (Washington: United States Institute of Peace Press, 1996).

S. Han, 'Building a Peace that Lasts: The United Nations and Post-Civil War Peace-Building', *Journal of International Law and Politics,* vol. 26 (Summer 1994), pp.843-867.

J.W. Harbeson, 'Democratisation and Conflict Resolution in Sub-Saharan Africa : A Research Agenda', presented at the tri-annual meeting of the *International Political Science Association* (Seoul, August, 1997).

M. Harbottle, 'The United Nations and its Capacity for Keeping the Peace', *Fellowship Briefing*, no. 4 (November 1984).

J. Heininger, *Peacekeeping in Transition: The United Nations in Cambodia* (New York: Twentieth Century Fund Press, 1994).

S. Hoffmann, 'The Crisis of Liberal Internationalism', *Foreign Policy*, no. 98 (Spring 1995), pp. 159-179.

K. J. Holsti, 'Legacies of Imperialism: Post-Cold War Analyses of Armed Conflict in the Peripheries', presented in the tri-annual meeting of the *International Political Science Association* (Seoul, August 1997).

S. Huntington, 'The West: Unique, Not Universal', *Foreign Affairs*, vol. 75 (November-December 1996), pp. 28-46.

M. Ignatieff, *The Warrior's Honour: Ethnic War and the Modern Conscience* (Toronto: Penguin, 1997).

International Centre for Peace Initiatives, 'Staff Report on Building Peace Through Good Governance', *Peace Initiatives*, vol. 3 (1997).

International Institute of Strategic Studies, *The Military Balance 1997-98* (Oxford: Oxford University Press, 1997).

R. Kaplan, 'The Future of Democracy: Was Democracy Just a Moment?' *The Atlantic Monthly*, vol. 280 (December 1997).

C. Kaufmann, 'Possible and Impossible Solutions to Ethnic Civil Wars', *International Security*, vol. 20 (Spring 1996), pp. 136-175.

C. Kegley (ed.), *Controversies in International Relations Theory: Realism and the Neo-Liberal Challenge* (New York: St. Martin's Press, 1995).

R. Keohane and L. Martin, 'The Promise of Institutionalist Theory', *International Security*, vol. 20 (Summer 1995), pp. 39-51.

C. King, 'Ending Civil Wars', *Adelphi Papers*, no. 308 (March 1997).

J. King, 'A Hindrance to Peace: Small Arms and Light Weapons Proliferation in Post-Conflict Peace Process', *Peacekeeping and International Relations*, vol. 26 (July-October 1997).

K. Kumar, *Rebuilding Societies After Civil War: Critical Roles for International Assistance* (Lynne Rienner, 1997).

W. Kühne, *Winning the Peace: Concept and Lessons Learned of Post-Conflict Peacebuilding* (Ebenhausen: Research Institute for International Affairs, July 1996).

J. P. Lederach, *Building Peace: Sustainable Reconciliation in Divided Societies* (Washington, D.C.: Unites States Institute of Peace Press, 1997).

R. Licklider, 'The Consequences of Negotiated Settlements in Civil Wars, 1945-1993', *American Political Science Review*, vol. 89 (September 1995), pp. 681-690.

M. T. Love, *Peacebuilding Through Reconciliation in Northern Ireland* (Aldershot: Avebury, 1995).

M. Lund, 'Early Warning and Preventive Diplomacy' in Chester A. Crocker, Fen Osler Hampson et al. (eds), *Managing Global Chaos. Sources and Responses to International Conflict* (Washington: United States Institute of Peace Press, 1996).

M. Mandelbaum, 'Foreign Policy as Social Work', *Foreign Affairs*, vol. 75 (January-February 1996), pp. 16-32.

E. Mansfield and J. Snyder, 'Democratisation and the Danger of War', *International Security*, vol. 20 (Summer 1995), pp. 5-38.

D. McLean, *Peace Operations and Common Sense, Replacing Rhetoric with Realism,* no. 9 (Washington, D.C.: United States Institute of Peace Peacework, 1996), pp. 1-4.

J. Mearsheimer, 'The Only Exit From Bosnia', *New York Times* (October 7, 1997), pp. A-13.

T. Milburn, 'A Framework for Assessing New Zealand Peacekeeping', *Peacekeeping and International Relations*, vol. 26 (March-April 1997), pp. 3-9.

Minister Lloyd Axworthy, 'Canada and Human Security: The Need for Leadership', *Statements and Publications* (Ottawa: DFAIT, December 1996), pp. 1-2.

Minister Lloyd Axworthy, speech given at York University, 'Building Peace to Last: Establishing a Canadian Peacebuilding Initiative', *Address* #96/46, Department of Foreign Affairs and International Trade (North York, Ontario: October 30, 1996).

L. Neack, 'Peacekeeping's New Dark Age', presented at the annual meeting of the *International Studies Association* (Toronto, March 1997).

R. de Nevers, 'Democratisation and Ethnic Conflict', *Survival*, vol. 35 (Summer 1993), pp. 31-48.

Open-Ended Working Group on An Agenda for Peace (June 10, 1996).

R. Paris, 'Peacebuilding and the Limits of Liberal Internationalism', *International Security*, vol. 22 (Fall 1997), pp. 54-89.

B. Posen, 'The Security Dilemma and Ethnic Conflict', *Survival*, vol. 35 (Spring 1993), pp. 27-47.

E. Regher, *Rebuilding Peace in War-Torn and War-Threatened Societies: The Challenge of Peacebuilding* (Ploughshare's Monitor, 1995).

M. Renner, 'Transforming Security', in L. Brown, *State of the World 1997* (New York: Norton, 1997), pp. 115-131.

J. F. Rioux and R. Hay, 'La convergence entre développement, paix at sécurité', *Note de recherché* (Montréal: Raoul-Dandurand, 1997).

W. Robinson, *Promoting Polyarchy: Globalisation, US Intervention, and Hegemony* (New York: Cambridge University Press, 1996), p. 457.

J. G. Ruggie, *Winning the Peace: America and World Order in the New Era* (New York: Columbia University Press, 1996).

J. M. O. Sharp, 'Dayton Report Card', *International Security*, vol. 22 (Winter 1997-98), pp. 101-137.

T. Shaw, 'Beyond Post-Conflict Peacebuilding: What Links to Sustainable Development and Human Security?' *International Peacekeeping*, vol. 3 (Summer 1996).

J. Shear, 'Bosnia's Post-Dayton Traumas', *Foreign Policy*, no. 104 (Fall 1996), pp. 87-101.

A. de Soto and G. del Castillo, 'Obstacles to Peacebuilding', *Foreign Policy*, no. 94 (Spring 1994), pp. 69-83.

S. J. Stedman and D. Rothchild, 'Peace Operations: From Short-Term to Long-Term Commitment', *International Peacekeeping*, vol. 3 (Summer 1996), pp. 17-35.

S. J. Stedman, 'Spoiler Problems in Peace Processes', *International Security*, vol. 22 (Fall 1997), pp. 5-53.

S. J. Stedman, 'Alchemy for a New World Order: Overselling "Preventive Diplomacy"', *Foreign Affairs*, vol. 74 (May-June 1995), pp. 14-20.

S. J. Stedman, 'The New Interventionists', *Foreign Affairs, America and the World 1992-1993*, vol. 72 (Spring 1993), pp. 1-16.

58   *Introduction*

J. Stremlau, 'Antidote to Anarchy', in Brad Roberts (ed.), *Order and Disorder after the Cold War* (Cambridge: MIT Press, 1995), pp. 397-412.

N. Tschirgi, 'Defending Peacebuilding', DFAIT-NGO *Peacebuilding Consultations* (Ottawa: DFAIT, February 7, 1997).

The Economist, 'The Rulers, the Ruled and the African Reality' (September 20, 1997), p. 49.

United Nations, *The Blue Helmets: A Review of United Nations Peacekeeping*, 3rd edn (New York: United Nations Department of Public Information, 1990).

S. Van Evera, 'Hypotheses on Nationalism and War', *International Security*, vol. 18 (Spring 1994), pp. 5-39.

T. Weiss and C. Collins, *Humanitarian Challenges and Intervention. World Politics and the Dilemmas of Help* (Boulder: Westview Press, 1996), pp. 13-38.

T. Weiss and L. Gordenker (eds), *NGOs, the UN and Global Governance* (Boulder: Lynne Rienner, 1996).

S. Willett, 'Ostriches, Wise Old Elephants and Economic Reconstruction in Mozambique', *International Peacekeeping*, vol. 2 (Spring 1995).

F. Zakaria, 'The Rise of Illiberal Democracy', *Foreign Affairs*, vol. 76 (November-December 1997), pp. 22-43.

Part II: Peacekeeping and Capacity Building

3 Peacekeeping Strategies for Peacebuilding: Multi-Functional Roles

Ho-Won Jeong

Since failure to control renewed violence prevents the reconstruction of a relationship among former antagonists, peacekeeping is an essential component of peacebuilding in the countries, which re-emerge from civil war. Due to a low level of trust between former adversaries, the role of a third party in monitoring the implementation process is critical. The presence of international observers helps change a climate of mutual distrust and suspicion. Peacekeeping is also blended into non-military aspects of post-conflict reconstruction activities at both operational and functional levels.

A peacekeeping role has to be more than maintaining a status quo; its functions have been extended and have become more context specific beyond the elements considered to be central to a traditional operation. Its operational goals now include the protection of minorities and other segments of a civil society and institution building as well as prevention of violence. In the areas of governance, peacekeepers may have to confront local authorities that are corrupt or repressive of minority groups in order to promote long-term stability and democratisation within troubled states.

With a paradigm shift, the success of peacekeeping is more seriously considered in terms of its long-term impact on reconstruction of violence torn societies. The responsibilities of peacekeeping campaigns for post-conflict reconstruction have been expanded from physical security to community building. In support of the restoration of justice, public administration and development, peacekeeping has to adopt different rules and become engaged in non-traditional military activities. In fulfilling their expanded mandates, collaboration with United Nations (UN) specialised agencies, international aid agencies and grassroots groups has become a critical factor in the success of any mission's operations.

This chapter investigates the ways in which short-term peacekeeping has evolved to long-term peacebuilding interventions. The recent experiences of multinational missions can be identified in terms of peace enforcement, maintaining civic order and trust building. In addition, the chapter examines conditions under which peacekeeping can contribute to constructive community-based peacebuilding.

PEACEKEEPING ROLES FOR PEACEBUILDING

Traditional peacekeeping roles of maintaining a cease-fire between borders of adversarial states (reflected in the UN Emergency Force during the Suez crisis and Interim Force in Lebanon, 1978) have been replaced by an emphasis on the control of violence at a communal level where the central authority does not function properly or its legitimacy is challenged (Hillen, 2000; Otunnu, 1998). Peacekeeping for the management of inter-group conflict within a state is a departure from traditional peacekeeping during the Cold War era, which served as a mechanism to prevent the dangerous escalation of the regional conflicts to superpower confrontation by controlling local conflict (Coulon, 1998). In contrast with the traditional operating environment where there are clear buffer zones, the new generation of peacekeeping has to be adapted to internal conflict situations where community boundaries have been re-created. The tasks faced by UN forces in Somalia and the North Atlantic Treaty Organisation (NATO) Stabilisation Force (SFOR) in Bosnia and other missions in the Balkans have been complicated by inter-communal conflict.

Peacekeeping missions have become more complex and diverse since their goals and mandates have to fit in an overall framework of a peacebuilding process. Starting with the 1989 Namibia operation (considered the forerunner of other post-Cold War peacekeeping missions) and in the following missions in El Salvador, Guatemala, Cambodia and Bosnia, greater attention has been paid to election monitoring, public administration, human rights protection and other civilian aspects of peacekeeping. The UN Observer Group in Central America (ONUCA) was mandated for police monitoring, the repatriation of refugees, the resettlement of displaced persons and provision of humanitarian assistance.

The mandate of the UN Angola Verification Mission (UNAVEM) I was limited to monitoring the withdrawal of the Cuban troops in 1988-89 whereas the mandate of UNAVEM II (dispatched following the Bicesse Accords in 1991) was expanded and enlarged to observe the elections. The UN Observer Mission in Angola (MONUA), replacing UNAVEM III in 1997, strengthened political and human rights staff in the field while reducing the number of military observers (Hare, 1998). Supervising the demobilisation of armed groups drew more serious attention in the UN Operations in Mozambique (ONUMOZ) from 1992 to 1994.

The UN Operation in Somalia (UNOSOM) II between 1993 and 1995 can be considered one of the most comprehensive missions along with those for Bosnia and Cambodia. In addition to providing security for the supply of humanitarian assistance, helping the return of refugees and internally displaced people and enforcing the arms embargo, the mission also was engaged in demining for rehabilitation, setting up a local administrative structure, and re-establishing both the police force and justice system (Halim, 1997).

Prior to the Namibia operation, an international presence did little more than freezing the status quo without effective local peacebuilding initiatives. In their traditional roles, peacekeepers who were deployed as lightly armed troops did not have to expose themselves to the direct conflict between adversaries since their main role was to monitor military activities of separated troops (Debrix, 1999). In this minimalist approach, a mission's success is judged in terms of maintenance of regional stability by controlling violent conflict situations.

Some international interventions such as the UN peacekeeping missions in Cyprus and Lebanon have been prolonged due to a fear of the consequences of withdrawal in the absence of a serious reconciliation process. Maintaining a cease-fire proves insufficient to bring about positive conditions for peace if that is solidified as a status quo. In fact, it may well be argued that long-lasting missions can effectively freeze the conflict by providing parties with a cost effective alternative to another cycle of violence.

Military roles become no longer monolithic with the demand for a multiplicity of functions, and military patrols for ensuring compliance with a cease-fire agreement are not considered enough (Boutros-Ghali, 1998). Some missions are limited to disarmament, demobilisation of former combatants and the enforcement of arms embargo, but others become involved in arresting war criminals (Moxon-Browne, 1998). While peacekeeping contributes to negative peace through maintaining law and order, it can support positive peace for promoting conditions for rehabilitation and reconstruction.

FUNCTIONS OF PEACEKEEPING

The social environment has to be stabilised through the control of violence. This is a necessary condition for not only reduction in inter-ethnic hatred but also for the increase in inter-community travel or communication. Re-establishing inter-communal links requires a secure environment for free movement of people across boundaries. The challenges faced by peacekeeping include social instability and violence resulting from the population move and competition for resources. Peacekeeping often operates in communities where a significant percent of the pre-war population is dead or displaced. The return of refugees and internally displaced people, de-mining, supply of food and shelter are crucial for rehabilitation and reconstruction.

As a traditional distinction between peacekeeping and peacemaking is blurred in a post-conflict peacebuilding context, peacekeeping lies on the interface between a police function and problem solving. Overcoming the experiences of a violent conflict should not be separated from reducing mistrust. Since fear of recurrent violence prolongs international presence, successful conflict resolution is part of an exit strategy for peacekeeping. Thus conflict resolution and reconciliation capacity has to be integrated into a peacekeeping mission.

Restoring order is not effective with military forces alone, since soldiers do not operate in isolation from a large social and political environment. In failed states where a functioning government broke down, the challenge 'far goes beyond controlling violence' (Last, 2000, p. 84). Peacekeeping has to provide support for functions of public service where the administrative structure collapsed (for example, Kosovo, Bosnia and Haiti). Government and civil society have to be supported to counter violence and to meet the requirement of an effective justice.

The environment for peacekeeping operations is affected by the process of rebuilding a political structure, of reconciliation and of reform of judicial and police institutions. At the same time, peacekeeping action can have an impact on identifying and supporting structures that will strengthen and solidify stable relations between former adversaries. By maintaining good relations with different factions, peacekeepers can facilitate a process, which allows the negotiation of a new institutional framework.

While peacekeeping is still more directed at conflict management, the success of peacekeeping is judged now more in terms of how it supports other policy instruments designed for addressing root causes of violent conflict. Control of violent behaviour for personal and community security is only part of a large approach to peacebuilding. Relief, development and human rights are all related to enhancing human security. A traditional focus centred on state security is obsolete for personal security and the rights of civilians.

OPERATIONAL GOALS AND ENVIRONMENT

Operationally, peacekeeping is often dispatched prior to the formulation of policies for reconstruction of war torn societies, and its main aim is to maintain order and provide essential public functions and services until a new infrastructure is built. The UN peacekeeping involvement, as seen in Cambodia and other countries, is largely concluded by the establishment of a new government following the holding of national elections. The scope of peacekeeping operations can be narrowed due to competition for limited resources which are, to a great extent, attributed to the dramatic increase in the number of authorised peace operations over the last decade, along with the shift in international attention from inter-state war (for example, Arab-Israeli War and Iran-Iraq War) to violent ethnic conflict.

In general, the complexities in the function of the military differ according to its mandate. Operational modes differ between monitoring activities and logistical support for elections and administration. The missions deployed as part of confidence building strategies can operate with a small contingent not overburdened by multiple roles. Forces oriented toward enforcement intervention require a larger size to confront challenges from local militias, as is illustrated by the United Task Force (UNITAF) in Somalia. International intervention in protracted conflicts requires sufficient force to control an extreme faction.

The proper size and capability of the force should be considered, in part, in terms of 'the degree to which the parties are prepared to cooperate with each other' (Last, 2000, p. 84). While a lack of cooperation from rebel forces required stronger enforcement components, the UNAVEM II did not have the capacity to support the implementation of the comprehensive nature of the 1991 Bicesse Accords, including integration of both government and rebel armies and internationally monitored elections in Angola. On the other hand, ONUMOZ was in a much stronger position to accomplish the demobilisation of government and Resistencia Nacional Mocambicana (RENAMO) soldiers and elections with more than 8,000 troops, military observers and civilian police.

The application of peacekeeping is affected by not only an external but also internal environment. In contrast with peacekeeping before the late 1980s, which relied on contributions from a handful of small and neutral states, the size of the new missions has been expanded along with broadening activities (Magyar and Conteh-Morgan, 1998). Owing to the involvement of more countries and differences in training and staff procedures among national contingents, a command and control structure has become inevitably complicated (Olonisakin, 2000).

The failure to arrest warlord Mohamed Farah Aidid by UNOSOM II is ascribed to poor planning as well as a lack of clear political goals. The ambush of a Pakistanis contingent sent to inspect an arms depot led to the involvement of US troops in the operation to capture Adid. However, the tangled command arrangements of UNOSOM II, ascribed to the American refusal to put its troops under foreign command, significantly contributed to a disastrous outcome with the death of eighteen American soldiers (Coulon, 1998). In addition, while UNOSOM II had over-confidence in firepower and heavily relied on military activities, they ignored a local contact and did not have support from the population.

Such factors as ambiguous policy goals, lack of clear policymaking structures and local political uncertainties have an impact on the conduct of peacekeeping operations. Working in an uncertain social and political environment is not easily adaptable to the traditional military operations whose main targets are clearly defined enemies. A lack of information about local communities can also cause difficulties in planning for tactical actions and insufficient operational knowledge.

Overall, degrees and types of intervention depend on force levels, its size and structure as well as the availability of international resources and support. A stable strategic and operational environment, especially oriented toward community building, is crucial for the success of an entire mission. Local support is critical for the accomplishment of nation building tasks such as the establishment of district and regional councils. On the other hand, it is not feasible to get consent for intervention in collapsed states where humanitarian needs have to be met.

Improving Relations with Civilian Components

Multiple points of interface between the civilian and military components require collaboration between peacekeepers and aid workers. Military aspects of peacekeeping are often overwhelmed by the demand for non-military services. Military forces, by default, take on the civilian tasks such as humanitarian relief and public administration. In peace support operations, the military occasionally have to take on similar tasks done by a relief agency with the emergency provision of water and medical care (Fishel, 2000; Wilkinson, 2000). A command structure has to be adapted to supporting the needs of parallel functions performed by a multitude of actors.

Both the military and civilian operations have markedly distinctive training programmes, patterns of decision-making, and attitudes toward authority. In military operations, the rules of engagement provide guidance for all parts of the structure (from senior decision makers to soldiers on the ground). The military have clear and well-defined lines of authority with its hierarchical structure, while civilian operations are decentralised with an emphasis on consensus decision making. The military chain of command does not help develop a collaborative relationship with civilian agencies, which have relatively flat authority structure. Compared with military operations, which have to articulate mission objectives before actions, NGOs have an ability to act without detailed planning, thus more easily adjusting to the challenge of sudden humanitarian needs. Due to their informal management style, NGOs also have an advantage of working through personal engagement.

Despite the demand for a more integrated approach to multi-dimensional peacekeeping and its impact on other agencies' work, 'a unified concept of operation' seldom exists (Last, 2000). For instance, from the onset, the military and civilian components of UNOSOM II had different perceptions of each other's roles. The military believed that civilian agencies ought to support the enforcement of order, whereas the civilian agencies perceived that the military's role should be supplementary to their task of delivering aid.

Although the lack of unity is less problematic 'during traditional peacekeeping operations in which soldiers have had little to do but maintain a buffer zone', peace operations will be marginally successful without mutual agreements on basic questions of means and ends of the mandate (Mockaitis, 1999, p. 136). Technical, logistical and security concerns are interwoven when military forces and relief agencies work in the same fields for providing food, water and health care or rebuilding transformation systems. It is essential for military units and civilian agencies in the field to co-ordinate their actions at a tactical level, especially when they help the same population and pursue similar objectives (Slim, 1997).

There are a variety of models to co-ordinate the relations

between peacekeeping missions and civilian authorities. A liaison officer can be appointed for a civilian commanded humanitarian co-ordination office. The military can support a mission headquarters run under the direction of the lead agency such as UNDP (for example, the operation in Rwanda in 1994). In the UN Transition Assistance Group (UNTAG) in Namibia, dispatched in 1989-90, military components were subordinate to a single Head of Mission.

In the absence of an effective civilian administrative structure, local diplomacy becomes largely the military's responsibility. For instance, the force commander of UN Protection Force (UNPROFOR) in Bosnia (1992-1995) assumed a diplomatic and a public relations role since no ranking civilian counterparts stayed in Sarajevo. When co-ordinating efforts are not effective at the higher level, individual national contingents can co-ordinate military support for food distribution and the security of UN compounds. In Somalia, Australian forces established their own civil-military operation team in order to manage relations with local elders, NGOs and UN political officers (Williams, 1998).

PEACE ENFORCEMENT

The enforcement function is designed to stabilise a fragile security situation especially when intervention is required to protect human lives (Albaugh, 2000; Herbst, 2000). The presence of peacekeeping is aimed at reducing the level of violence by deterring the continued use of violent strategies. Thus peacekeepers cannot simply be bystanders in fighting between armed groups. In the absence of reconciliation, peaceful co-existence is based on a precarious balance. Unlike their earlier counterparts applied to a cease-fire for an inter-state war, intra-state peacekeeping missions cannot simply withdraw from the outbreak of new violence. The withdrawal of peacekeepers from Rwanda, in response to the escalation of violence organised by Hutu extremists, allowed mass killing (Niva, 1999). Defence of unarmed civilians is a military responsibility accepted by an international humanitarian law (Gray, 2000; Shraga, 2000).

Peacekeeping and enforcement functions should not be seen as distinct activities but as a point on a continuum (Mockaitis, 1999). UN forces are authorised to use force not only for self-defence, but also to accomplish their assigned missions (Cox, 1999; Jett, 2000). Neutrality has to be flexibly interpreted when international forces have to identify guilty individuals and communities and arrest war criminals. The consent of local parties is not technically feasible when force has to be employed against violent local elements such as the Khmer Rouge in Cambodia (Gibbs, 2000).

In the event of recurrent violence, the principles of neutrality and impartiality have to be superseded by the principles of humanitarian intervention. Military forces can be used to guarantee the return of refugees as well as to protect convoys of goods and delivery of aid to people under attack (de Mello, 2001). In providing assistance, peacekeepers physically have to intervene in violent situations where local residents confront returnees with weapons.

National contingents are different in the coverage for the protection of populations and relief agencies. Faced with Serbian threats, Italian and some other contingents in the Bosnian operations even discouraged Muslim populations from visiting the grave of their family members rather than provide them with protection. The failure of peacekeepers to disarm militia groups left the re-establishment of new political institutions fragile and created an insecure environment for humanitarian assistance in Somalia.

In many situations, peacekeeping operations have been too cautious to respond to violent situations. In the enforcement of order, peacekeepers have to be ready to confront aggressors rather than reacting passively to the escalation of violence since the goal of intervention is maintaining peace. Western powers often take a half-hearted approach to controlling extreme local factions because of fear of casualties resulting from a military confrontation. Even Western officials conceded that the mess created in Bosnia is attributed to the reluctance to control extreme nationalist Croat and Serb factions, which resisted imposition of any rules. The former head of NATO forces in Bosnia suggested the exaggeration of risks involved in helping the transformation of former Yugoslavia by Western politicians (*The Washington Post*, November 25, 2000).

In reality, enforcement is likely to be considered in terms of the balance between the extent to which the toleration of violence leads to obstruction of a peace process and the circumstances, which make the use of force too costly or difficult. In precarious political situations, there is always a danger of peacekeeping being dragged into uncontrollable local situations without much preparation.

POLICE FUNCTIONS AND INSTITUTIONAL SUPPORT

In providing internal security, dealing with unorganised mob violence requires different approaches since its nature differs from threats caused by paramilitary organisations, which attempt to initiate a full-scale civil war. In response to violence targeted against individuals and small groups (for example, Kosovo Albanians against Gypsies and Serbs following the withdrawal of Federal Yugoslav army), international peacekeepers perform a police function in order to protect property and basic rights of minority groups. In maintaining order, police functions rely less on the explicit use of force and coercive tactics and more on cultivating (or fostering) local support. Military doctrines become either irrelevant or inappropriate to promoting personal and communal security.

If the goal of a mission is not a victory over enemies but the maintenance of law and order at a community level, policing skills are more relevant than combat skills. In controlling unorganised mob violence, a minimal use of force is required not to provoke violent resistance. Mob violence using rocks and Molotov cocktails demands different operational responses. In this situation, shouting and shoving are more helpful than shooting. The use of force, if it is inevitable, has to be gradually and reluctantly introduced.

Since combat units, trained in the use of overwhelming force, are not effective in responding to riots or other civilian disturbances, specially trained units are necessary to perform police functions. Military police are better prepared for street patrols and are more skillful in interacting with the population. Compared with infantry troops, they are the least likely to fire first even under beleaguered situations. Combat units, trained to kill enemies, can be abusive with civilians without proper training. This is well illustrated by the example of US Airborne paratroopers who were accused of their brutality in the Kosovo operation (*The Washington Post*, March 25, 2001). International military forces are deployed to preserve order, before 'civilian police are gradually reintroduced.' (Last, 2000, p. 89). Soldiers serve as the public security force and reduce the domestic security gap by restoring law and order because local police members do not have enough experience. Peacekeeping controls the paramilitary to ensure security of all citizens while 'a national police must be organised, trained and equipped with the ability to provide public security' (Garver, 1997, p. 3). Thus international military intervention is 'an incomplete solution to physical security shortfalls without incorporating effective police elements' (Last, 2000, p. 87).

Peacekeeping roles have been taken by non-military units with the increasing use of international civilian police. For instance, the nature of UNTAG in Namibia was originally considered as military operation (Hearn, 1999). The mission, however, soon turned into a mixed military-civilian operation with the increase in the number of Civilian Police (CIVPOL) monitors at the expense of military personnel.

By the mid-1990s, peacekeeping operations had been succeeded by the missions focused exclusively upon police institution building as is illustrated by the UN Civilian Police Mission in Haiti and the UN Police Support Group in Eastern Slovenia. The UN support mission in Haiti de facto abolished the military and ended the domination of the military over civil and political life, with the creation of a professional civilian police force. Designing and training a new civilian police force in Haiti became one of the first UN operations that stressed police development in its mandate. The UN Observer Mission in El Salvador (ONUSAL) provided valuable logistical, training and monitoring support for the creation of the new national civil police, which replaced the earlier police dominated by the military with a previous history of human rights abuses. In El Salvador, CIVPOL monitored human rights abuses and helped recruit, screen and train a completely new police force (Holm and Eide, 2000)

In general, the police role was initially confined to crime prevention and maintenance of public order without the power to investigate crimes. As reviewed above, CIVPOLs also undertook a task from advising, training and screening to supervising local police. In the election process, CIVPOL monitored the activities of the Mozambique police unit to prevent intimidation and respect for human rights. In Eastern Slovania and Bosnia, CIVPOL monitored agreements to integrate ethnic minorities into the police. Civilian police units in peacekeeping operations for Cambodia had a capacity to enforce law and order of UN political authority as well as monitor the work of the local police force. While providing public security as part of the unusual UN assumption of some state functions, the international mission even arrested suspects for charges brought by a special UN Prosecutor.

Rebuilding legal and social institutions needs to be supported by community policing. The exercise of a police function requires the framework of a fair and effective judicial system. International missions provide training on community policing and human rights as well as monitoring local police. While providing assistance in the restructuring of the police, the military force can be used to shut down police stations in the events of local police violating the agreement. 'The international military force is the backup that helps to force violence down to levels where effective civilian police can handle it' (Last, 2000, p. 84).

COMMUNITY BUILDING

For the purpose of conflict prevention, peacekeeping strategies include the promotion of collaborative relationships among groups with different interests (Borris and Diehl, 1998). Since the terms for reconciliation should be determined by the parties themselves, peacekeeping cannot impose attitudinal adjustments artificially. In social terms, however, peacekeeping offers neighbourhoods an opportunity to work together rather than find a reason to attack and defeat the opponent by bringing stability to the relationship.

The psychological assurance of not being attacked is the first step for re-establishing a renewed relationship, but it does not automatically translate into trust. The assurance of stopping violence does not provide a basis for building genuine trust if the separation of different groups into divided communities has to be perpetuated. In fact, as is illustrated by Bosnia and Cyprus, peacekeeping can inhibit reconciliation by reducing the need for direct interactions between separated communities. The operational goals of peacekeeping need to be more directly linked to building bridges between former enemies by encouraging co-operative endeavour.

Through their mediator roles, peacekeepers can facilitate non-violent resolution of conflicts, which accommodates opposing interests and needs (Druckman, et al., 1999). Peacekeeping field offices are filled with various personal and community level problems. While they cannot take all the individual cases, peacekeepers may have to mediate or arbitrate immediate property disputes between displaced people occupying others' houses and returnees. Socio-psychological methods can contribute to gaining insight into inter-group and inter-personal dynamics.

Handling violent situations requires special training for conflict resolution and third party intervention skills. Different skill-sets can be utilised in linking the control of violence to the repair of relationships. Peacekeeping can support a dialogue process arranged through peace commissions. Formerly hostile groups can be represented at various forums with logistical support provided by peacekeeping operations.

In order to maintain good relations with local communities, knowledge of local culture has become fundamental. Contingents have varying relationships with the local population, depending on their awareness of local social and cultural contexts. Military units can be deployed to a specific area for an extended period of time to learn how to work with local authorities more effectively and get to know local people better (Mockaitis, 1999). The knowledge of local society and culture can be used to help the efforts for peacebuilding from below.

Peacekeepers can operate as part of the local environment and become an active element in community building with the familiarity to indigenous cultural, political and social situations. The acquaintance with the local situation helps peacekeepers nurture contact with ordinary citizens and political elites in the areas where they are stationed. The subtleties of short-term alliances among local groups, the strength of kinship relationships and the nuances of religious differences are all important sources of operational knowledge for successful peacekeeping.

CONCLUSION

Peacekeeping missions have been re-designed as part of a transition strategy for social reconstruction. A one dimensional approach of peacekeeping (limited to supervising a cease-fire) would not be effective in overcoming formidable barriers for peacebuilding embedded in social and cultural conditions. To fit in a post-conflict settlement process, as we have seen earlier, peacekeeping functions have been modified and expanded to such areas as maintaining public order and providing logistical support for socio-economic programmes. Operational goals and activities vary according to diverse settings in which peacekeeping is introduced.

The modes of intervention such as the control of a warlord and maintenance of public order need to be based on the analysis of local conflict dynamics. In particular when the parties are willing to cooperate, less coercive methods can be more effective. Dealing with unarmed civilians requires restraints of force and conciliatory measures based on dialogue and mediation. The integration of peacekeeping roles into community building has to be supported by partnerships with the local population.

REFERENCES

E. A. Albaugh, 'Preventing Conflict in Africa: Possibilities of Peace Enforcement', in Robert I. Rotberg (ed.), *Peacekeeping and Peace Enforcement in Africa* (Cambridge: World Peace Foundation, 2000).

E. Borris and P. F. Diehl, 'Forgiveness, Reconciliation and the Contribution of International Peacekeeping', in H. J. Langholtz (ed.), *The Psychology of Peacekeeping* (Westport: Praeger, 1998), pp. 207-222.

B. Boutros-Ghali, 'Peacemaking and Peacekeeping for the New Century', in Olara Otunnu (ed.), *Peacemaking and Peacekeeping for the New Century* (Lanham: Rowman & Littlefield Publishers, 1998).

J. Coulon, *Soldiers of Diplomacy: the United Nations, Peacekeeping and the New World Order* (Toronto: University of Toronto Press, 1998).

K. Cox, 'Beyond Self-Defense: United Nations Peacekeeping Operations & The Use of Force', *Denver Journal of International Law and Policy*, vol. 27, no. 2 (1999).

S. V. de Mello, 'The Evolution of UN Humanitarian Operations', in D. S. Gordon and F. H. Toase (eds), *Aspects of Peacekeeping* (London: Frank Cass, 2000), pp. 115-124.

F. Debrix, *Re-Envisioning Peacekeeping: the United Nations and the Mobilization of Ideology* (Minneapolis: University of Minnesota Press, 1999).

D. Druckman, et al., 'Conflict Resolution Roles in International Peacekeeping Missions', in H. W. Jeong (ed.), *The New Agenda for Peace Research* (Aldershot: Ashgate, 1999).

J. T. Fishel, 'Beyond Jointness: Civil-Military Cooperation in Achieving the Desired End-State', in M. G. Manwaring and A. J. Jones (ed.), *Beyond Declaring Victory and Coming Home: The Challenges of Peace and Stability Operations* (Westport: Praeger, 2000).

R. Garver, *Restoration of Public Security: The Linchpin in Peacebuilding and Post-Conflict Operations* (Carlisle Barracks: U.S. Army War College, 1997).

D. Gibbs, 'The United Nations, International Peacekeeping and the Question of "Impartiality"' *The Journal of Modern African Studies*, vol. 38, no. 3 (2000), pp. 359-383.

C. Gray, *International Law and the Use of Force* (New York: Oxford University Press, 2000).

O. Halim, 'A Peacekeeper's Perspective of Peacebuilding in Somalia', in J. Ginifer (ed.), Beyond the Emergency (London: Frank Cass, 1997), pp. 70-86.

P. Hare, *Angola's Last Best Chance for Peace* (Washington, D.C.: US Institute of Peace, 1998).

R. Hearn, *UN Peacekeeping in Action: The Namibian Experience* (Commack: Nova Science Publishers, 1999).

J. Herbst, 'African Peacekeepers and State Failure', in Robert I. Rotberg (ed.), *Peacekeeping and Peace Enforcement in Africa* (Cambridge: World Peace Foundation, 2000).

J. Hillen, *Blue Helmets: The Strategy of UN Military Operations*, 2nd edn (Washington, D.C.: Brassey's, 2000).

T. T. Holm and E. B. Eide, *Peacebuilding and Police Reform* (London: Frank Cass, 2000).

D. C. Jett, *Why Peacekeeping Fails* (New York: St. Martin's Press, 2000).

D. Last, 'Organizing for Effective Peacebuilding', in T. Woodhouse and O. Ramsbotham (eds), *Peacekeeping and Conflict Resolution* (London: Frank Cass, 2000), pp. 80-96.

K. P. Magyar and E. Conteh-Morgan (eds), *Peacekeeping in Africa: ECOMOG in Liberia* (Houndmills: Macmillan Press, 1998).

T. R. Mockaitis, *Peace Operations and Intrastate Conflict: the Sword or the Olive Branch?* (Westport: Praeger, 1999).

E. Moxon-Browne, *A Future for Peacekeeping?* (Houndmills, Macmillan Press, 1998).

S. Niva, 'Peacekeeping, Indifference and Genocide in Rwanda' in Jutta Weldes (ed.), *Cultures of Insecurity: States, Communities, and the Production of Danger* (Minneapolis: University of Minnesota Press, 1999).

F. Olonisakin, *Reinventing Peacekeeping in Africa: Conceptual and Legal Issues in ECOMOG Operations* (Boston: Kluwer Law International, 2000).

O. A. Otunnu (ed.), *Peacemaking and Peacekeeping for the New Century* (Lanham: Rowman & Littlefield Publishers, 1998).

D. Shraga, 'UN Peacekeeping Operations: Applicability of International Humanitarian Law and Responsibility for Operations-Related Damage', *The American Journal of International Law*, vol. 94, no. 2 (2000).

H. Slim, 'Relief Agencies and Moral Standing in War: Principles of Humanity, Impartiality, and Solidarity', in D. Eade (ed.), *From Conflict to Peace in a Changing World: Social Reconstruction in Times of Transition* (Oxford: Oxfam GB, 1998).

H. Slim, 'The Stretcher and the Drum: Civil-Military Relations in Peace Support Operations', in J. Ginifer (ed.), *Beyond the Emergency* (London: Frank Cass, 1997), pp. 123-140.

M. C. Williams, 'Civil-Military Relations and Peacekeeping', *Adelphi Paper 321* (Oxford: Oxford University Press, 1998).

P. Wilkinson, 'Sharpening the Weapons of Peace: Peace Support Operations and Complex Emergencies', in T. Woodhouse and O. Ramsbotham (eds), *Peacekeeping and Conflict Resolution* (London: Frank Cass, 2000).

4 Negotiation Readiness in the Development Context: Adding Capacity to Ripeness

Bertram I. Spector

International development situations are rife with conflict. Societies receiving development assistance are usually undergoing dramatic changes to their social, economic and political fabric. These changes can alter the status quo and reapportion the stakes within civil society and between civil society and government, often yielding discord, and sometimes outright hostility and violence, among groups that perceive a loss of power or influence.

If these groups have both the political will and the capacity to defend and promote their interests, they may decide to negotiate their differences and prevent, manage or resolve the conflict. But in many cases, civil societies in developing countries have the motivation and will, but not a sufficiently mature capacity to negotiate, enabling differences to escalate into conflicts undeterred. A major consequence of such conflicts is distraction from or derailment of the initiating development activities and objectives.

This chapter examines these dynamics through the concept of 'negotiation readiness', which combines the motivation and willingness to negotiate (ripeness) with the capacity to negotiate with the external environment. Negotiation readiness adds to Zartman's concept of ripeness (1996), but is different from Pruitt's conception (1997). It is patterned on the concept of military readiness, which emphasises both the willingness and capacity to act or respond in armed conflict situations. Willingness and capacity are equally important in generating the decision to negotiate. If the disputing parties lack a sufficient level of capacity, they are not likely to decide to negotiate their differences, fearing a concessionary, or worse, an exploitative, interaction, even if they are motivated and the conflict seems ripe for resolution. Thus, capacity and ripeness are strategically linked and both must be present for parties to decide to negotiate.

Development situations examined in this chapter include situations in which policy reforms are being implemented. This context can produce conflicts among stakeholders. In this situation, the playing field may not be level: government usually maintains greater power and authority over reforms, while civil society is often factionalised and without a single voice to represent its position. Moreover, civil society often lacks the maturity and experience to demand an equal place at the negotiating table to determine the direction of future reforms.

The ability to reduce or resolve these conflicts and move forward with development goals depends on the ripeness and capacity of the parties, and their readiness, to negotiate. This chapter seeks to understand the centrality of this 'negotiation readiness' concept to successful development with implications for peacebuilding efforts. It puts forth the hypothesis that if parties lack sufficient negotiation readiness (that is, motivation and capacity), development and post-settlement peacebuilding efforts will suffer and may become deadlocked. On the other hand, if all parties involved in development or participating in implementing a peace agreement are ready to enter into negotiations concerning the implementation details, the results are more likely to be successful.

The essential thrust of this chapter is to understand the components, preconditions, situational impacts, and variability of negotiation readiness so as to be able to explain when parties feel comfortable enough to enter into negotiations and what might be done to stimulate or encourage parties to engage in negotiations. Drawing upon analogies to military readiness and referring to existing literature on negotiation ripeness and post-agreement negotiation, the chapter expands upon a framework that seeks to explain the decision to enter into negotiations (Spector, 1998). Several cases are presented to illustrate how readiness can be strengthened in development situations to facilitate the onset of negotiations. Finally, conclusions are drawn on how the concept of negotiation readiness might be elaborated theoretically and tested pragmatically.

CONFLICTS IN DEVELOPMENT SITUATIONS

Conflict almost always accompanies the implementation of policy change. Paradoxically, the implementation of policy change cannot proceed efficiently in an atmosphere marked by excessive or disruptive conflict. Thus, a necessary condition of implementing policy change effectively must be the design, development and institutionalisation of processes and structures that are capable of managing, if not resolving, disputes that threaten policy reform. Generating culturally-appropriate ways to overcome or, at a minimum, stabilise the effects of social conflict are important as well, in building indigenous capacity to apply, transfer and sustain conflict resolution and management processes and skills.

There are many opportunities for conflict to emerge in the process of implementing policy change. For example, conflicts can arise when there are attempts to change institutions and procedures; redistribute land, property and other resources; gain access to a backlogged court system; deal with bureaucratic gridlock; share power; relocate and resettle populations; and decentralise government. Disputes can emerge among stakeholders if they perceive the stakes to be high and their goals are incompatible or their interests clash. These disputes can concern either conflicts over policy objectives or disagreements over the means to carry out the policy (Matland, 1995). In extreme situations, aggrieved stakeholders may withhold their resources or actions that are required to implement policy or actively sabotage attempts to reform policy, engendering disruptive power struggles.

The very tasks that comprise policy implementation are fraught with potential conflict, both within and among stakeholder groups (Crosby, 1996). Table 1 examines the breadth of implementation tasks and the types of disputes that might be generated in accomplishing them.

Table 1. Policy Implementation Tasks and Potential Disputes

Policy Implementation Tasks	Potential Disputes
1. **Policy Legitimation.** The proposed policy initiative must acquire legitimacy in the eyes of those who will implement it.	• Legitimising a new policy may antagonise stakeholders that oppose it and upset the status quo, yielding conflict.
2. **Constituency Building.** The policy must be marketed and promoted to build an identifiable coalition of beneficiaries.	• Those likely to lose from implementation of a new policy may form a counter-force to the likely beneficiaries.
3. **Resource Accumulation.** Resources supporting the capacity to implement the policy must be obtained or reallocated.	• Reallocation of limited resources usually results in curtailing of old policies.
4. **Organisational Design and Modification.** Institutions must be reengineered or developed anew to be appropriate to the new policy.	• Existing organisations usually need to be reoriented, displacing groups and individuals associated with the old policy.
5. **Resources Mobilisation.** Resources must be redirected to provide the capacity to conduct action plans.	• Redirecting resources can cause resistance from those who lose capacity.

A common theme across all of these tasks is the uncertainty caused by implementing policy change and the potential for loss of status and resources. These negatively viewed circumstances elevate the probability for conflict among the possible winners and losers.

In pluralistic societies, both the formulation and implementation of policy change almost always evoke debate among governmental and nongovernmental groups that have conflicting interests concerning the issues at hand. However, implementation managers who remain alert to the context of policy reform -- both the goals of reform and the levels of potential stakeholder conflict -- will be better equipped to preempt or react quickly to the impediments to change that emerge with appropriate dispute resolution remedies (Matland, 1995). Certainly, when there is a general consensus favoring the implementation of certain policies, such as a health program to eradicate smallpox, there may be only minimal disputes.   Implementation in these cases can be relatively straightforward technical activities, possibly hampered by resource availability or bureaucratic skill and motivation, but not by substantive disputes over the policy itself (see Table 2). Some view implementation under these conditions as an *administrative* function of putting regulations and legislation into effect (Cell 1). However, even in a case of administrative implementation, conflicts may arise regarding resource distribution and differences in implementation approach across the technocratic groups that are entrusted with executing the policy.   These conflicts may be resolvable by building confidence levels among stakeholders or by accommodating resource allocation needs.

Table 2. Goal Ambiguity-Conflict Matrix: Policy Implementation Processes

Ambiguity	**Low Conflict**	**High Conflict**
Low Goal Ambiguity	1. Administrative Implementation	2. Political Implementation
High Goal Ambiguity	3. Experimental Implementation	4. Value-Laden Implementation

(Adapted from Matland, 1995)

Clear goals ('low ambiguity') and high conflict among stakeholders usually yield a highly *political implementation* situation (Cell 2). In such cases, actor goals or methods are incompatible with the proposed policy and political power must be wielded to resolve the impasse. This can result in the coercive use of power to impose a solution or in persuasive interactions among stakeholders involving negotiation or joint problem-solving. Examples of political implementation might include controversies over the demobilisation and relocation of guerrillas or the opening or closing of military bases.

The conditions defined in Cell 3, high goal ambiguity and low conflict, define many typical implementation scenarios in which development objectives are vague and open, but are relatively unthreatening; only limited groups in society are interest-motivated toward these objectives and no conflicts among them are generated as a result. Those who perceive a high personal stake in the issue and who get involved actively will play a dominant role in executing the policy. An example is the implementation of forestry policies or clean air or water regulations. The outcome depends heavily on the resources committed and the stakeholders who decide to participate. As a result, implementation is likely to vary from site to site and can be viewed as *experimental*, producing lessons learned at each site that can enhance future implementation activities.

Finally, the situation in Cell 4 -- high ambiguity and high conflict -- is typical of the implementation of issues dealing with *highly salient symbols*, those that deal with the essential values, principles and goals that stakeholders espouse. Conflict may arise over the 'correct' vision of policy orientation on these issues, resulting in significant competition among groups and possible disruption of efficient implementation processes. An example of this type of implementation, especially among environmental stakeholders, is the siting of hazardous waste treatment plants. When the clash of strongly held beliefs dominates policy implementation, the dispute resolution techniques that are mobilised must be sensitive to the needs and values of the stakeholders, not only to their interests. Several conditions or sources of conflict can generate resistance from expected implementers, as well as from beneficiaries:

1. *Absence of Consensus.* If the policies to be implemented are based on issues where there is limited consensus in society, conflict may emerge. Interested parties in government agencies, industry and society who are charged with responsibility for implementation or who must be relied upon to comply with a new policy may not agree with the substance of the policy or the means employed to implement it. In fact, the policy change may pit government authorities against other governmental and nongovernmental organisations that have conflicting interests on the issues. When policies remain contentious after their formulation due to remaining legal, political, social or economic questions, compliance with new policy may suffer and, worse yet, the implementers may try to obstruct it.

2. *Challenge to the Status Quo.* Stakeholders may find a new policy to be a direct challenge to their interests. They may fear that they will lose status, influence or assets as a result of a reformed policy, and so, may resist change by withholding their resources and failing to comply with the policy's requirements. A change in the status quo implies upsetting the existing power balance, arrangement of coalitions or distribution of assets and resources. Policy change is likely to introduce new issues, new actors, and new regulations and standards, producing a sense of uncertainty and risk in an established situation by redefining who are winners and who are losers. If stakeholders weigh their options and determine that they are better off *without* the policy -- to stay with the status quo -- they are likely to oppose or resist the change. This cost-benefit assessment may be more intuitive than quantitative.

3. *Adversarial History.* If the policy-making and implementing communities are historical adversaries, the implementation period may be characterised by conflict. Any proposed change in policy, regardless of its technical merit, may be seen as an offensive gesture, dredging up old enmities and wounds between historical adversaries. Regardless of the interests of the parties in the policy issues at hand, implementation may be viewed as just another opportunity to confront the other side.

4. *Exclusion.* When policy makers have shut out parties with potentially competing viewpoints from participating in the policy formulation phase, the implementation phase is a likely moment for their frustrations to be released. Such constituencies may have weak allegiances to the new policy. The imposition of new regulations or directives on parties that have been denied access during the initiation of policy dialogue is likely to be viewed negatively and responded to by questioning, delay, outright hostility or stalemate.

When disputes manifest themselves publicly, there are several possible consequences. Public resistance can emerge, resources can be withheld, implementing activities can be delayed, or the process can become hopelessly deadlocked. Worse yet, social and political unrest concerning one policy issue can spiral and trigger other conflicts, producing increasingly unstable situations.

A particular variant of development conflicts concerns dynamics in post-conflict peacebuilding situations. Here, again, conflicts may arise and negotiation may be required. The implementation of peace agreements are extremely sensitive junctures that determine whether the provisions that have been agreed upon at the negotiating table can be successfully 'sold' to the constituents who must enact them. Time and again in the Israeli-Palestinian conflict, for instance, agreements concluded through negotiation at the highest political levels fall asunder because constituents who must implement the peace provisions have not 'bought on'.

Research suggests, that the more detailed the negotiated peace agreement, the more likely the implementation will have the intended consequences (Hampson, 1996). However, formal settlements to conflicts often include broad framework provisions, but remain silent on many of the important details. They define the basic modalities by which the fighting will cease, the various factions will be disarmed, and reconciliation, institution-building and reconstruction will begin -- all vital elements that usually require more implementation details. Many peace agreements, sometimes consciously and sometimes unconsciously, leave major details concerning their implementation unresolved or ill-defined, bequeathing these problems to the parties in the peacebuilding phase. Without detailed answers to such questions as safe havens, amnesties, demilitarised zones, weapon drop-off locations, agreement on neutral parties to administer disarmament, interim arrangements, elections, administration of essential services, rule of law, human rights, reestablishment of the judiciary, reestablishment of the economy, and so on, peace agreements can easily fall apart and renewed conflict can emerge.

The provisions of post-conflict peacebuilding, often promoted and sponsored by bilateral and international donor organisations, can radically alter power arrangements, thrusting certain groups into authoritative positions before they gain local legitimacy or the capacity to lead. The very circumstance of post-conflict peacebuilding is one in which established power balances in society are overturned and the reestablishment of orderly functioning relies on different groups or coalitions assuming new roles. Unless this new order is imposed autocratically, instability and unrest are likely to emerge during peacebuilding until there is common acceptance of the new arrangements or the newly empowered groups gain the resources and abilities to provide credible leadership.

NEGOTIATION READINESS IN DEVELOPMENT CONFLICT SITUATIONS

The principal mechanism to generate answers to such development conflict quandaries is *continued* negotiation among the disputants. When there are conflicts of interest over development issues, the parties can seek equitable resolution through dialogue and negotiation. Especially in the case of post-conflict peacebuilding situations, it is through formal and informal *post-agreement negotiation* among these parties that sensitive details can get resolved, sometimes with the help of outside mediators.[1] These post-agreement negotiations serve not only to implement the peace agreement or other policy changes, but as a conflict management mechanism in often unstable and transitional post-conflict periods.[2] But are disputants always capable of negotiating the details? These details may have been sticking points in peace negotiations which is why they were not resolved earlier. The parties still may view them as intractable and non-negotiable now. The success or failure of development and post-settlement negotiations depends largely on the *negotiation readiness* of the parties. Negotiation readiness can be defined as the combination of *political willingness* and *capacity* of parties to decide that it is in their best interest to negotiate an agreement rather than to continue the conflict. If any of the principal parties are not ready to negotiate, development or peacebuilding may come to a halt and conflict may reemerge.

While Zartman's 'negotiation ripeness' and Pruitt's expanded versions of the concept, focus on the motivational willingness to enter into talks as well as on perceptual elements, the concept of negotiation readiness proposed here adds another critical dimension of 'capacity', which, in development situations, may prove to be even more important to the decision to negotiate. Policy change disputants may be willing to negotiate the details of implementation, but may lack the tools, training and resources to adequately represent themselves at the bargaining table, especially if it is after years of prolonged conflict or suppression of civil society. This political skill or capacity gap can result in a critical asymmetry of political power among the parties, potentially yielding a potent disincentive to negotiating implementation. There may be a need to level the playing field among civil society groups and government with regard to their capacity to sit down at the bargaining table and negotiate solutions that all believe to be equitable and fairly achieved. The efficacy of donor assistance to strengthen civil society organisations may turn out to be the critical required element in generating negotiation readiness.

Ripeness

By identifying and analysing ripe moments, 'ripeness theory' seeks to understand and explain the fundamental decision to enter into negotiations. Zartman stipulates four basic conditions for establishing the ripeness to negotiate: (1) the existence of a *mutually hurting stalemate* or impending *catastrophe* that causes all parties to conclude that escalation is no longer an option and that deadlock is too costly; (2) alternatively, the existence of *mutually enticing opportunities* that offer rewards for negotiation that are too good to turn down; (3) a *perceived way out* of the conflict that does not sacrifice the parties' basic interests; and (4) valid and legitimate spokespersons who can commit their parties to the negotiation path (1989, 1996). Zartman's ripeness concept is primarily a motivational construct.

Pruitt has recently critiqued 'ripeness theory' and has sought to incorporate it within the goal/expectation model of strategic choice (1997). He questions whether ripeness is a state or a variable, in which there could be degrees of ripeness. He also questions whether ripeness relates only to entering into negotiations or if it suggests the conditions for effective negotiations themselves. To satisfy these issues, Pruitt proposes 'readiness theory', his extension to ripeness theory. It recategorises the ripeness conditions into two categories -- the *motive* to achieve mutual cooperation and *optimism* that the other parties will reciprocate cooperative behaviour -- thus adding perceptual to motivational dynamics in the theory.

Readiness

One critical element is missing in these frameworks of ripeness or readiness that is extremely important in development and post-conflict negotiations, and that is *political capacity*. Making analogy to 'military readiness' may serve to inform our development of a 'negotiation readiness' framework. What does it mean to be ready militarily? The indicators used by US military forces focus on four factors: personnel, equipment and supplies in hand, the condition of the equipment, and training (Gebicke, 1997). All of these are factors that measure the resources and capacity to do a job, in this case, to conduct combat. Also included in an assessment of military readiness are the threats to be confronted, the appropriateness of the resources to those threats, and the 'connective tissue' that makes this capacity viable -- communications, coordination and planning. While there is still much debate on how military readiness should be measured (is it a snapshot state or dynamic? is it short-term or long-term? how do different missions affect readiness? etc.), its emphasis on the *capacity* of the parties can help expand our concept of negotiation readiness.

Motivation and perception are not sufficient to ensure the decision to negotiate; the parties must possess a degree of political skill, resources and power -- some reasonable level of capacity -- if negotiations are to be entered into and conducted effectively. These skills and resources must go beyond a group's military capacity, by which they may have waged their struggle until the peace agreement, to a capacity to act and represent their interests in a civil situation. The parties must have a sense of political identity and structure, be able to establish their interests and develop strategies, and possess persuasive and tactical skills. But in a developing or post-conflict society, civil organisations are often underdeveloped or nonexistent. Institutions and societal rules and procedures may have to be reestablished. Reconciliation, reconstruction and institution-building require active negotiation among all stakeholders who have interests, motivation and a capacity to sit and react at the bargaining table. Power and resource asymmetry between the disputants will likely result in a failure to enter into talks and possible stalemate in peacebuilding or policy change efforts.

Referring to the propensity of ethnic groups to negotiate with the state to avert the growth of conflict, Rothchild emphasises the importance of developing at least the perception or appearance of symmetry between the parties to motivate negotiations (1997). Ethnic groups that are in a less powerful position in relation to the state are not likely to be interested in peacebuilding negotiations unless the state takes initiatives to equalise the balance of power, to empower the ethnic groups and to enhance their political capacity. This might take the form of power sharing or confidence building measures. He cites South Africa as a good example of engaging ethnic groups in negotiation through such initiatives that leveled the playing field.

The following questions suggest the issues that need to be addressed to provide substance to a 'negotiation readiness theory'.

- What are the components of negotiation readiness and the decision to enter into negotiations?
- What are the necessary and sufficient conditions for a party to be ready? Are there degrees of negotiation readiness?
- How ready do parties have to be to decide to enter negotiations in a development or post-conflict situation?
- What are the preconditions for sufficient readiness? How much motivational ripeness versus perceptual optimism versus political capacity need there be?
- What are the likely consequences if all parties are not ready to negotiate?
- Are there situational or intervening factors that may impact negotiation readiness?
- Can something be done to stimulate the negotiation readiness of parties and thus make development and peacebuilding efforts more effective? What are the ways to enhance or stimulate negotiation readiness?
- How do the motivational and perceptual factors in ripeness theory interface with the resource, capacity and experience factors of readiness?
- How can the concept of military readiness inform the development of a negotiation readiness framework?
- What types of external support can enhance capacity building for development or peacebuilding negotiations?
- What are the implications for foreign donor assistance in post-conflict situations?

ILLUSTRATIVE EXAMPLES

Three examples are presented below that depict cases where international donors, foundations or institutes have supported institutional strengthening of civil society to enhance their negotiation readiness. These illustrations focus on situations in which policy changes are being implemented in the development context. In all cases, the strengthening of negotiation skills is seen to have favorable short-term results; long-term implications for the resolution of conflicts are more difficult to ascertain.

The West African Enterprise Network

Since 1992, over 300 business people in 12 West African countries have worked together as an Enterprise Network to seek policy change in their countries by strengthening their organisational and planning capacity and increasing their skills in advocacy (Orsini and Courcelle, 1996). Their goal is to enhance their dialogue with the State concerning business- and economic-related policy issues in which they are major stakeholders. Prior to establishing the Network across the 12 countries, the private sector maintained poor relations with the State. There was general mistrust, limited mechanisms for dialogue and unequal power positions. Businesses were typically dependent on 'favours' from the State, subject to restrictive regulations, and hostage to corrupt and rent-seeking bureaucrats. The business sector needed extensive capacity strengthening to participate as an equal partner in the policy process.

The means chosen for achieving greater capacity was through development of skills in strategic management (including techniques such as stakeholder analysis and political mapping) and advocacy (including techniques to help formulate interests and positions, organise around these interests, articulate and promote these interests with government, lobby, use the media, provide public testimony and build coalitions). Strategic management skills are directly applicable to pre-negotiation situations, in which stakeholders need to analyse their own interests and contrast them with the interests of the other negotiators, plan their course of action, and strategise how they will carry out the negotiation process. Advocacy skills are valuable in promoting stakeholder interests effectively vis à vis the State, negotiating and using persuasive tactics and applying various resources (such as the press) to one's advantage.

Through training sessions, workshops and other interventions geared to strengthen the capacity of the Network members in negotiation-usable skills, the Network has begun to play an important negotiating and advisory role in many of the constituent counties. For example, in Ghana, the Network is consulted regularly as the representative of entrepreneurs in reforming economic policy. In Mali, the Network is asked by the government and legislature to give advice on proposed legislation and to negotiate with the Finance Committee on fiscal reform issues. In Senegal, the Network negotiates with government on post-devaluation business incentives. Across the other countries, the Network negotiates with the States on policy reform concerning access to credit, banking regulations, investment, tax reform and regional economic integration.

The Ugandan National Forum

In 1989, the Implementing Policy Change Project (sponsored by the US Agency for International Development [USAID]) began working with both public and private sector groups in Uganda to develop an atmosphere for stimulating private investment, expanding exports, strengthening the financial sector and creating an equitable tax regime (Kalema, Mazzie and Ojoo, 1994). One important and concrete result of that work -- and an illustrative example of 'dispute management systems' -- was the establishment of the National Forum on Strategic Management for Private Investment and Export Growth in 1992. The Forum was conceived as a sustainable body for dialogue, problem-solving and negotiation among various governmental and industry stakeholders to develop consensus toward specific action plans that promote investment. The Forum, by combining the forces of the private sector in one organisation, serves to enhance the power and capacity of businesses to negotiate with the government. It draws its legitimacy from the support it receives from the President of Uganda and from the Uganda Manufacturers Association. Four working groups that meet continuously on specific issues strengthen the links among stakeholders and serve as a ready outlet for anticipating, managing, negotiating, and resolving disputes among them. Several broad issues have been addressed by these working groups that carry the seeds of dissensus, including shifting control over the economy away from government to the private sector; privatising public enterprises and increasing competition; restructuring several government agencies; and dealing with corruption and developing a plan for land reform. Each of these issues threatens to change the status quo, redistribute resources and restructure who in society exercises economic power -- all sensitive issues that can easily divide stakeholders and yield disputes. Not only do these working groups support consensus-building internally among stakeholders, but they help to forge unity among them by serving as externally-focused pressure groups on government, offering policy recommendations to government agencies and following through on implementation monitoring to ensure that reforms are made.

Ukrainian Negotiation Training for Government Managers

Negotiation and consensus-building training is being provided to government managers in Ukraine through the Ukraine Public Administration Academy (with the support of the USAID's Implementing Policy Change Project). While different from the previous two cases in that the target of institutional strengthening here is government rather than civil society, the case is relevant because it demonstrates the importance of developing a strong capacity in negotiation skills to promote policy reforms. On many fronts, but especially in the realm of the economy, Ukrainian policy reform has come to a virtual standstill because the various government ministries and agencies that must collaborate with one another do not have the skills or experience of negotiating with each other over competing organisational interests to develop mutually acceptable policy provisions. The problem also is prevalent within the legislature and between the legislature and the executive agencies. Under the socialist system, the decision-making culture had developed as a centralised, top-down model; decisions were made and passed to implementing agencies, not negotiated. With the breakup of the Soviet Union, this decision model has also changed, but the negotiation skills have still not developed sufficiently to fill the void, resulting in deadlock. It is hoped that the negotiation training program will begin the process of enhancing the capacity of these agencies and institutions to search for common ground on important policy issues.

CONCLUSIONS

From a theoretical perspective, the expansion of the ripeness concept to the readiness concept, by adding the capacity element to the motivational and perceptual elements, makes it more responsive to development situations and generates better explanations for why parties decide to negotiate. Especially in post-conflict peacebuilding situations, the negotiation readiness concept can offer a more realistic explanation of why certain peace agreements experience successful implementation and why others fail. Asserting the ripeness of a conflict, by itself, is not sufficient to predict the onset of negotiations; the parties must have the practical capacity to negotiate as well.

From a policy perspective, the concept of negotiation readiness immediately suggests that donor assistance might be well spent to enhance the capacity of civil society and government in negotiation skills. Especially in sensitive post-conflict situations, international donors might have a major impact on improving the chances of a peace agreement by channeling their support to negotiation and conflict resolution training activities that help empower civil society groups and make them more capable of joining in post-settlement implementation negotiations as equal partners.

NOTES

The author gratefully acknowledges the support of the Jacob and Hilda Blaustein Foundation.

1. The importance of such post-agreement negotiations, especially at the local level to facilitate implementation, has been described and analysed by Evans, Jacobson and Putnam (1993) in the context of security, economic and North-South issues, and by Spector, Zartman and Sjöstedt (forthcoming) to assess the dynamics of regime governance and expansion processes.

2. The use of the negotiation mechanism as a form of conflict management and implementation of already negotiated agreements is only recently receiving attention by the research community, mostly as it relates to sustaining international regimes. Lodge (1998), for example, examines negotiation processes as consensus-building and regime governance mechanisms within the European Union. Spector, Zartman and Sjöstedt (forthcoming) analyse six international regimes to highlight the use of negotiation processes both at the domestic and international levels to iron out the details, implement, and expand upon the originating regime agreements. Putnam (1988) and Evans, Jacobson and Putnam (1993) examine the two-level game -- the domestic bargaining that ensues to implement internationally negotiated agreements consummated by national signatories. What these studies conclude is that implementation of even the most carefully crafted agreements requires additional negotiation if they are complex multi-issue agreements. The development of dynamic and cooperative processes of post-agreement negotiation offers the basis for interested parties to bargain on the details and complexities that could not be resolved in the originating agreement. Such after-the-fact negotiation also offers the possibility to modify and expand upon agreement provisions that, with the course of time, should be enhanced.

REFERENCES

D. Chigas, 'Unofficial Interventions with Official Actors: Parallel Negotiation Training in Violent Intrastate Conflicts', *International Negotiation*, vol. 2, no. 3 (1997).

Creative Associates, Inc., *Preventing and Mitigating Violent Conflicts: A Guide for Practitioners*, Principal Author: Michael Lund (Washington, D.C.: Creative Associates Inc., 1996).

B. Crosby, 'Policy Analysis Units: Useful Mechanisms for Implementing Policy Reform', *Implementing Policy Change Working Paper No. 10* (Washington, D.C.: Management Systems International, October 1996).

P. Evans, H. Jacobson and R. Putnam (eds), *Double-Edged Diplomacy* (Berkeley: University of California Press, 1993).

M. Gebicke, 'Military Readiness–Improvements Still Needed in Assessing Military Readiness', Testimony before the Subcommittee on Military Readiness, Committee on National Security, U.S. House of Representatives (11 March 1997), GAO/T-NSIAD-97-107.

F. Hampson, *Nurturing Peace: Why Peace Settlements Succeed or Fail* (Washington, D.C.: United States Institute of Peace Press, 1996).

W. Kalema, B. Mazzie and Z. O. Ojoo, 'Status Report: National Forum on Strategic Management for Private Investment and Export Growth', Implementing Policy Change Project Series (Washington, D.C.: Management Systems International, 1994).

J. Lodge (ed.), 'Negotiations in the European Union: Special Issue', *International Negotiation*, vol. 3, no. 3 (1998).

S. Low, 'The Zimbabwe Settlement, 1976-1979', in S. Touval and I. W. Zartman (eds), *International Mediation in Theory and Practice* (Boulder: Westview Press, 1985).

R. Matland, 'Synthesizing the Implementation Literature: The Ambiguity-Conflict Model of Policy Implementation', *Journal of Public Administration Research and Theory*, vol. 5, no. 2 (1995), pp. 145-174.

D. Orsini and M. Courcelle, 'The West African Enterprise Network', Case Study No. 4, *Implementing Policy Change Project Case Studies Series* (Washington, D.C.: Management Systems International, October 1996).

D. Pruitt, 'Ripeness Theory and the Oslo Talks', *International Negotiation*, vol. 2, no. 2 (1997), pp. 237-250.

R. Putnam, 'Diplomacy and Domestic Politics: The Logic of Two-Level Games', *International Organization*, vol. 42 (Summer 1988), pp. 427-460.

D. Rothchild, 'Ethnic Bargaining and the Management of Intense Conflict', *International Negotiation*, vol. 2, no. 1 (1997), pp. 1-20.

B. I. Spector, 'Deciding to Negotiate with Villains', *Negotiation Journal*, vol. 14, no. 1 (January 1998).

B. I. Spector, I. W. Zartman and G. Sjöstedt (eds), *Getting It Done: Post-Agreement Negotiation and International Regimes* (forthcoming).

I. W. Zartman, *Ripe for Resolution: Conflict Resolution in Africa*, 2nd edn (New York: Oxford, 1989).

I. W. Zartman, 'Bargaining and Conflict Resolution', in E. Kolodziej and R. Kanet (eds), *Coping with Conflict after the Cold War* (Baltimore: Johns Hopkins University Press, 1996).

Part III: Reconciliation and Social Rehabilitation

5 Reconciliation: Contexts and Consequences

Charles Lerche and Ho-Won Jeong

In the aftermath of intense struggles, especially violent ones, there is a need to reverse the negative relationship dynamics involving factionalised identity groups who have to live in close proximity to each other (Lederach, 1997, pp. 13-15). Hearts and minds are ravaged by war and violence, and their healing is as critical a need as the reconstruction of burnt out towns or villages. True peacebuilding must include strategies to assist antagonists to get beyond their past violence and estrangement. In this context, the main focus of reconciliation is to create new perceptions and explore new shared experiences, thereby changing key relationship dynamics in the conflict system.

Though most analysts and commentators agree that reconciliation focuses on bridging the gap and healing the relationships between alienated groups, they are not so clear as to whether there is one reconciliation or many. For those who see the phenomenon as essentially the same at all levels, groups and nations can be healed through similar processes as individuals. However, others see reconciliation in the context of political transition. One may also ask whether reconciliation is an end or a means; or whether it is a process or an outcome. In filling a variety of roles in post-conflict society, reconciliation does take, and has taken, diverse forms. We see it attempted and carried out on a variety of levels by various means; from small encounter groups, to high profile truth commissions, to apologies of top politicians for past wrongs. It may be politically neutral in one context and perceived as quite ideological in another. Or it may seem rather conservative in orientation and effect in one country, and quite transformative in substance and implication in a neighboring land. Whereas psychological approaches primarily stress 'harmony and cooperation', political approaches are essential to the analysis of deep structural divisions in a transitional society.

This chapter discusses different formulations of what reconciliation does and how it works. Since interactive workshop approaches are not easily transferred to a national setting, the role and functions of truth commissions need to be critically examined. On the one hand, psychological approaches to reconciliation tell us much about bridging the gap and healing relationships between alienated groups. On the other hand, the more political approaches reflect the dynamics of political order in transitional societies. Lastly, we make a case for *transformative* approaches to reconciliation.

RECONCILIATION AS PERSONAL HEALING

Violence, perceived injustice and negative stereotyping have combined over extended periods of time to render many contemporary conflicts inaccessible to standard non-violent resolution processes. Montville, who has studied the psychological effects of political violence in some depth, explains that those who have suffered unjustified violent attacks have an enduring fear of their trauma re-occurring; a fear which undermires the possibility of developing renewed trust in their victimisers, and inhibits any true negotiation or eventual (re)integration with them (Montville, 1998). Thus, in regard to most communal conflicts, time does not 'heal all wounds'. Instead, grievances associated with unacknowledged and unforgiven wounds are passed down the generations, creating a widening gap of estrangement, fear and hatred, which increases the likelihood of further violent conlict and aggravates its intensity. In these situations violence, either latent or manifest, has become the status quo and any lasting improvement can only come through changing the dynamics underlying this status quo.

Reconciliation is promoted by its theorists and practitioners as just such a tool of transformation, that can be conceptualised as a 'process of developing a mutual conciliatory accommodation between antagonistic or formerly antagonistic persons or groups'. Specifically, it 'refers to establishing a relatively amicable relationship' following infliction of extreme psychological and physical injury (Kriesberg, 1998, p. 184). The goal is to move the relationship beyond a cycle of revenge and retaliation through releasing negative emotions arising from past incidents (de la Rey, 2001; Meninger, 1996).

The significance of reconciliation is further underlined by an appreciation of how the trauma left behind by large-scale violence is passed from one generation to the next, perpetuating cycles of violence. Conflict, which is deeply rooted in culture and consciousness, has its own affective dynamics, fostering militarism and the 'glory' of killing the 'other' (Galtung, 1998a, p. 3). While despair, historical falsification, stereotyping, and dehumanisation affect the behaviour of the victims, distrust and indifference characterise the offenders' mental world. Reconciliation, therefore, has to change these organising principles which determine the way people choose to act in order to de-legitimise violence as a means for dealing with conflict (Lumsden, 1999, p. 3).

Since expectations about the future have an impact on the behaviour of the parties, hope needs to be generated by the projection of a brighter future. The systematic dehumanisation of victimised group(s) has to be reversed through psychotherapeutic treatment. Power imbalances between perpetrators and victims need to be redressed through a process of healing. This far reaching agenda requires the help of a variety of professionals -- social workers, therapists and artists, among others -- to assist all involved to acquire both the motivation and the skills necessary to correct past wrongs through symbolic, legal and material means.

True healing, according to Montville, can only come through reconciliation which involves a sequence of three steps:

1. *Acknowledgement.* When oppressors publicly acknowledge what they have done, knowledge becomes, in a sense, truth, and victims are assured (at

least to some extent) that the past will not repeat itself. This in itself contributes to victims' healing and thereby facilitates dialogue. However, 'the act of acknowledgment to be effective must be complete and detailed. The victim cannot accept the omission of any painful episode of loss by the acknowledging side, otherwise the good faith of the acknowledgment will be suspect' (Montville, 1998a).

2. *Contrition*. The next step is to take responsibility for past actions, to express regret, and directly request forgiveness. Again, sincerity, as judged by the victims, is the key to the success of this step.

3. *Forgiveness*. The first two steps by the oppressor/aggressor prepare the ground for the final psychological step, which is the victims' voluntary forgiveness of past injuries. It may take time for victims to express their forgiveness, but true acknowledgment and contrition by the other side will in themselves have a positive effect on relations between the parties (Montville, 1998a).

As explained here, acts of contrition start with the recognition of guilt and acceptance of responsibility, particularly for events, which have become symbols of inter-personal or inter-communal relations. Genuine forgiveness does not take place if anger and resentment are denied or ignored, though it does not necessarily assume an attitude of superiority or self-righteousness (Casarjian, 1992). The above three elements are essential in order for victimised groups to be reassured that they will not suffer the same abuses in future (1993, p. 113).

THE WORKSHOP

Whereas religious, ideological or other objective differences may still remain as conditions of future conflict, the interactive processes of reconciliation are based on the assumption that conflict dynamics are affected by such subjective factors as misperceptions, mistrust, and frustrated basic needs (Fisher, 1999). Genuine dialogue and conflict analysis of a mutual, interactive nature are essential to full, successful reconciliation between antagonistic groups. To create new relationships, social space is needed where people can recount their experiences and share perceptions and feelings with one another through an encounter. Montville and others envision this occurring in specially designed 'workshop' contexts where participants from both sides feel secure, and trained neutral third parties conduct various therapeutic exercises such as 'walks through history' (Henderson, 1996). In order to establish trust, participants should be able to 'openly recognise and accept responsibility for the actions of their side that caused hurt -- physical, psychological, moral -- in the other' (1999, p. 98).

A workshop approach is not, therefore, resigned to political realism's 'pessimistic inevitability' of recurring widespread violence. Rather, conflict is viewed as an 'interactive' process, driven as much by 'collective needs and fears' as by rational calculation of power and interests (Kelman, 1997, p. 194). John Burton's work, which highlights such basic needs as security, identity and social bonding has demonstrated that influencing these subjective factors can, in fact, change a negative political and psychological climate dominated by hostility, fear, pessimism and cynicism. Changes in perception, feeling and opinion can, in turn, bring about behavioural changes. In a situation where parties are still suspicious of each other, the workshop process is explicitly designed to achieve step-by-step progress until confidence is restored.

PUNISH OR PARDON?

What has been considered effective at the interpersonal level has also been attempted at the collective level. However, truth commissions, apologies by political figures to whole peoples or countries, or even war crimes tribunals, are simply not the same as problem solving workshops -- primarily because there is no guarantee that Montville's three stages of reconciliation will be experienced. As several recent cases illustrate, it is one thing to make known that the army or the police engaged in widespread human rights abuse. However, it is quite another thing to come to common agreement about what that means. In such a context, there may not be just one truth, but rather, many truths. Neither the Apartheid South African security forces nor the Latin American generals ever relinquished the belief that their fight to protect national security against Communist subversion justified the use of extreme measures, ordinarily incompatible with the principles of civilised governance.

Besides varying interpretations of what happened, there is also the vexed question of amnesty/impunity. If perpetrators escape the legal consequnces of their acts in exchange for public truth telling, then an orderly progression through Monville's three steps may become impossible, with the consequence that reconciliation remains, at best, incomplete. For instance, a former government interrogator, motivated by the possibility of amnesty, might well admit to and feel regret for a given act of torture, and even apologise for the pain it caused; but still maintain that, in context it had to be done. Such a scenario would represent, somewhat paradoxically, contrition without full acknowledgment of an act's wrongness.

Also, at the national level, in the context of a heavily publicised truth commission or the equivalent, real forgiveness is by no means guaranteed to occur. Many other reactions have appeared as well. Therefore, though there seems to be much agreement that knowing what happened is a necessary condition for forgiveness, it is certainly not a sufficient condition. There are also situations where forgiveness, and even the whole discourse of reconciliation are not yet possible or even appropriate. Consider, for instance, the situation in Rwanda in the immediate wake of the genocide, or in Sierra Leone as the truth about mass slaughters and childhood soldiers came to light. In short, we can not deny that 'knowing', as such, is just as likely to make some people more angry not less, more unwilling to let go of what they have suffered rather than to forgive. Consider, in this regard, the Madres de la Plaza de Mayo. They have continually rejected all government efforts at reconciliation which did not include complete legal investigation of every 'disappearance' in Argentina and full punishment for all those responsible for carrying them out. It is worth noting, however, that although they have gone on to espouse a variety of social justice issues, the Madres have not prevented a general acceptance of the government's grant of impunity to military officers involved in the excesses of the former regime.

Reconciliation should foremost accommodate the need of the victimised communities to reaffirm their sense of identity which has been threatened and denied. Such people can, and perhaps should, be encouraged to forgive; but they must also feel free to express their sorrow, anger and resentment in other ways meaningful to them. Above all, reconciliation cannot, in the name of 'national unity', impose closure on those not ready to forgive. Otherwise, there is a distinct possibility of national truth-telling resulting in 'false reconciliation'. Describing such a syndrome in Latin America, Ignatieff warns that:

> The societies in question used the truth commissions to indulge in the illusion that they had put the past behind them. The truth commissions allowed exactly the kind of false reconciliation with the past they had been expressly created to forestall (1996).

Any such equivocal public exercise can actually become an excuse to stop reflecting on the real meaning of recent events, and thereby stifle the energy and motivation to come to terms with what they really represent. Ignatieff argues further that the 'attitude that it would be proper for everything to be forgiven and forgotten by those who were wronged' inevitably undermines and corrupts reconciliation's real purpose (1996).

Truth-telling, by itself, is not really an adequate response to victims' demands for justice; some commissions have certainly not served adequately as means to other legitimate responses to the truths they brought to light. Rather, the question has arisen as to whether truth commissions can actually replace courts in redressing human rights abuses. The record might lead us to ask whether reconciliation is really about justice, in the usual sense of the term; and, if so, what kind of justice? Further questions arise in relation to the issue of reparations. Victims should certainly be compensated: but who should pay what to whom, and, most importantly, under what circumstances? Montville's formula would seem to indicate that those who have commited abuses should pay something as an act of contrition, even if it is largely symbolic. In practice, though, what restitution there has been has come from the sucessor governments. Even if motivated by good intentions, such gestures may raise serious questions of equity in the minds of victims when what they receive is compared to the full pardons enjoyed by the representatives of the old regime.

This issue has been raised in connection with the South African Truth and Reconciliation Commission, where to some extent, the impression was given that perpetrators gained more through amnesty than victims did through reparations. In Chile as well, the reparations did not compare with what might have been obtained if victims had been permitted to seek full legal redress -- something prevented through granting impunity to the military. Similar assessments have been made of the reparation regimes in Argentina, El Salvador and elsewhere (Edelstein, 1994). Since full compensation for this sort of suffering is really impossible, it seems that reparations inevitably seem like a 'buy off' for victims' complicity in the reconciliation process.

It is disturbing and somewhat ironic that national reconciliation programmes, in theory designed to redress terrible wrongs, might themselves raise serious questions about justice and equity. While admitting that new governments in post-conflict societies have enormous challenges to face, it is still hard to imagine the eventual emergence of a true human rights culture without a balanced use of both political and legal means. Short of this, the evidence suggests that in transitional societies lingering doubts about justice will tend to obscure the link between truth-telling and real reconciliation.

Efforts to punish wrong doers in the name of both retributary justice and future deterrence have certainly been limited by the realities of transitional politics. In countries where the new government consists largely of members of the former ruling class, such as El Salvador or Guatemala, it is very difficult indeed to follow a conventional legal route to justice. Therefore, several new regimes, trying to avoid the dangers inherent in confrontation with the 'old guard', have granted amnesty to them because it was politically convenient, despite the fact that political accountability for human rights violations is very likely critical for a successful political transition. If, as seems likely, the decision to 'pardon or prosecute' is made on political grounds because new governments have been unable or unwilling to bring perpetrators to court, then a truth commission is certainly better than nothing. The Guatemalan case typifies this problem since, as Wilson writes

> a maximalist 'Nuremberg option' for addressing war crimes is not even remotely possible in Guatemala. This is not to say that the legal route to justice should be abandoned altogether...What is essential is that the limitations of the legal system be recognised so that the Commission and other initiatives can complement its work (1997).

The international community can, and has to some extent, become more directly involved in resolving some of these issues through implementing international human rights norms and procedures. Special international tribunals, and particularly the newly created International Criminal Court, can reinforce national commitment to bringing violators to justice and to avoiding such excesses in the future. These developments go beyond institutional reform to influence the political culture within which new democratic institutions exist and function, and which is their real basis for reform and progress.

THE POLITICS OF RECONCILIATION

The insights of reconciliation have grown out of a deep dissatisfaction with traditional power and interest approaches to conflict that have not had much impact on cycles of violence, and it can be argued that reconciliation is really more 'realistic' than traditional *realpolitik* which omits the subjective dimension of experience (Montville, 1998, p. 2). The literature on reconciliation actually downplays, or even ignores, politics. Also, oddly enough, though it highlights the importance of the past, it also seems to be somewhat ahistorical in orientation: reconciliation is presented more as a discrete event than as a key process to insure the success of historical transition under less than ideal conditons.

Reconciliation has diverse functions and roles in the reconstruction of divided societies and the meanings of reconciliation at a national level can be contrasted with its meaning at lower levels. At an individual and group level, as we have seen, it aims at helping the victims overcome feelings of alienation and dis-empowerment, creating conditions for communal bonds. However, once one moves from the interpersonal to the collective and public level, all such efforts in the name of reconciliation *inevitably* have a political dimension. In fact, Hamber and van der Merwe have introduced the notion of *ideologies of reconciliation*, suggesting that several of the key participants in South Africa's post conflict experience have brought very different viewpoints and agendas to this aspect of peacebuilding (1998).

Post-conflict regimes need to increase their legitimacy and support by distancing themselves from their predecessors, and in this regard reconciliation is quite expedient. A few countries have, with some success, followed a policy of collective amnesia in the course of democratisation (Spain), but most other cases have followed the Latin American example of the 80s and 90s by going 'public' with the truth. While undoubtedly helpful, despite the limitations discussed above, one should not ignore the extent to which the political context shaped both the practice and consequences of national reconciliation. In this context, reconciliation has other goals besides forging social bonds between erstwhile antagonists. Truth commissions and similar practices are employed as means to consolidate new democracies by fostering national consensus around a goal of never experiencing human rights violations on such a scale again. It is essential that all political forces come to agree on the need to

> enhance social and political tolerance, to facilitate the institutionalisation (in the broadest sense possible) of democratic processes, to allow for transparency; to inculcate the notion of accountability amongst community members or citizens and their political leadership (Liebenberg and Zegeye, 1998, p. 544).

National reconciliation is, in other words, one element in a more comprehensive program to promote good governance in post-conflict society, which, in turn, will increase a new government's internal and external legitimacy and political capital.

Reconciliation should, in fact, lead to the emergence of effective on-going practices of conciliation in post-conflict society. Failing this, it is hard to see what prevents the cycle of alienation and conflict from starting over in the new political system, giving rise once again to efforts at reconciliation -- efforts that will be increasingly difficult for a disillusioned and exhausted public to take seriously. Ideally, effective mediation of interests of all social groups in an unequal, multi-ethnic society is made possible by transformation of existing relations between political institutions and society. Extensive effort in this direction have been made in some transitional systems. It is illustrated by the Guatemalan case:

> The central concerns of the peace accords include the need to transform existing relations between state and society, so that political institutions are capable, for the first time, of mediating the interests of all social groups in a poor, unequal multi-ethnic, and multilingual Guatemala. To achieve this transformation, core provisions express time and again the need for participative consultation in the formulation, execution, evaluation and monitoring of state policies, and for accountability in legislative action and executive decision-making (Prado, 1998).

In the 'real world' however, as well demonstrated in Guatemala and elsewhere, the road to these ideals is long with many obstacles and diversions; and in the tumultuous environment of transitional politics their realisation remains, at best, quite a long way off for the forseeable future (Prado, 1998).

In summary, mutual 'rehumanisation' of conflict protagonists is an important dimension of reconciliation, but it cannot be meaningfully separated from the broader task of political reconstruction. Reconciliation should not mean 'restoration', that is, putting back in place the past social arrangements or state of affairs. Rather, collective public sharing of past trauma should be a catalyst for the longer term task of reforging institutions and relationships among key political actors. In helping peoples to transcend the confrontations of the past, reconciliation can serve to generate new moral and political attitudes supportive of new political identitities free of exclusive ultra-nationalism.

SOCIAL CONFLICT AND SOCIAL JUSTICE

The problems of war-torn societies cannot be reduced to the conflict interface between victims and perpetrators. Van der Merwe tells us for instance that, 'the conflictual social system has a very direct impact on the way people come to define their interests and their ability to pursue them at a personal level' (1993, p. 270). Reconciliation cannot, therefore, avoid dealing with those ethnic and class issues which define groups and induce individuals or collectivities to move against each other. Inter-group competition for material and symbolic resources exists in all societies, and crops up along social 'fault lines' defined in terms of race, class, ideology, religion or language (Lane, 1994, p. 53). Since most resources are, by definition, scarce, the process of allocation always raises questions of distributive justice (Lane, 1994, p. 53). What distinguishes post-conflict societies in this regard is that violence, with all its dysfunctional and destructive consequences, has become an integral part of the allocatory process. So, though inter-group resource competition is central to political life everywhere, an overtly violent expression of this process indicates that a given set of institutions is incapable of effectively channeling and resolving the conflicts emerging from this competition.

The relations between any politically significant cleavage groups are not, of course, easily transformed from conflict into a state of harmony; but the conditions of peace do not necessarily require a state of absolute harmony. Rather, where conflict has degenerated into violence, the groups involved need to acquire 'the capacity to handle conflict creatively and non-violently' (Galtung, 1998b). Furthermore, if it is acknowledged that this type of inter-group relations has never existed in a given society, reconciliation then means more than psychological dimensions of conflict transformation; rather, it points toward social, political and economic reform on an unprecedented scale. Reconciliation seen from this perspective really calls an entire social system, and not just a particular inter-group relationship, into question.

Reconciliation also needs to focus on the socially disadvantaged, those who have been the most victimised by various forms of direct and structural violence. Socio-economic marginalisation and exclusion are often at the root of inter-group violence, and these dynamics do not necessarily change in post-conflict societies. A new social hierarchy leads underprivileged groups to search for a new form of social life often characterised by violence. For youth, in particular, the 'struggle' may simply shift from the politics of the street to street crime, as they find an identity and a place in gangs to replace what they had in political movements. This suggests that the violence of the past, rather than being purged through reconciliation, may be simply displaced into criminal activity.

The prevalence of violence and crime in a post-conflict environment highlights the fact that reconciliation is not enough by itself; other dimensions of peacebuilding such as economic reconstruction are essential to safely stabilise post-conflict society. Otherwise, class-related issues accentuated by the prescription of neo-liberal economic policies may bring on their own destructive conflicts. Therefore, omitting the welfare of marginalised groups runs the risk of leaving several of the root causes of violence and victimisation unacknowledged in the course of reconciliation.

There is a clear connection between patterns of structural violence and both interpersonal and inter-group conflict; and to the extent that reconciliation moves post-conflict societies away from such patterns, it should be seen as an instrument for creating positive peace. Thus, in the broadest sense, reconciliation's goal is to enhance justice based on the recognition and full acceptance of the supreme value of the human personality, through restoring the dignity of peoples from whom it has been stripped. In this sense, reconciliation is also a key element in fostering a culture of peace reflecting such values as truth, justice, mercy, and dignity. Ultimately, reconciliation represents a new form of adaptation; one of several our species must learn if it wishes to continue to exist. This adaptation requires, among other things, a critical examination of the effect of violence on our societies, our cultures and ourselves. For, as M. E. Clark has argued, 'only when social values and institutions are required to give account of themselves, when their fundamental assumptions are questioned, is there any hope of creating a political culture which fulfills rather than frustrates human needs' (1993, p. 51).

CONCLUSION

Reconciliation is a reaction to overt violence associated with widespread human rights abuse, but it is at the same time proactive in preventing conflicts of this kind. Reconcilation, through improved group relations, prevents further victimisation and dehumanisation. A logical, longer term outcome of reconciliation would be the elimination of the social conditions which have made it necessary in the first place.

As discussed earlier, national reconciliation cannot be limited to Montville's three steps of acknowledgment, contrition and forgiveness. Rather, justice has to figure into the process somewhere. However, it is precisely the inability of transitional democratic institutions to provide justice that constitutes the most compelling rationale for truth-telling alternatives. There is need to see reconciliation in a context where, instead of replacing or undermining retributive justice, it can potentially serve as a 'bridge' from a past where such justice was denied and a present where it is not yet practically and politically possible, to a future where, hopefully, it can become an integral part of the social order. In fact, the ambiguity about reconciliation arises from the transitional political context. National reconciliation, as a political exercise, may through 'coming to terms with the past', save the state but not necessarily heal the society; and post-conflict societies run the risk of exchanging political for criminal or structural violence. Unless specifically and directly addressed, violence will remain as a symptom of a violent culture.

Reconciliation should include the search for a model of governance and social relations that enables all groups in society to deal equitably and creatively with conflict. This is a long term project involving efforts to explore new institutions in both the public sector and civil society. Otherwise reconciliation will only be a stop gap measure necessitated because the government has not yet found the courage and commitment to assess their country's particular 'cultural pathologies'.

REFERENCES

I. Amadiume and A. Abdullahi (eds), *The Politics of Memory: Truth, Healing and Social Justice* (New York: Zed Books, 2000).

N. Biggar (ed.), *Burying the Past: Making Peace and Doing Justice after Civil Conflict* (Washington, D.C.: Georgetown University Press, 2001).

E. R. Borris, and P. Diehl, 'Forgiveness, Reconciliation, and the Contribution of International Peacekeeping', in H. J. Langholtz (ed.) *The Psychology of Peacekeeping* (New York: Praeger, 1998).

E. Boulding, *Culture of Peace* (Syracuse: Syracuse University Press, 2000).

R. Casarjian, *Forgiveness: A Bold Choice for a Peaceful Heart* (New York: Bantam Books, 1992).

M. E. Clark, 'Symptoms of Cultural Pathologies: A Hypothesis' in D. Sandole and H. van der Merwe, *Conflict Resolution Theory and Practice: Integration and Application* (New York: Manchester University Press, 1993).

Danish Institute of International Affairs (DUPI) *Humanitarian Intervention: Legal and Political Aspects* (Copenhagen: DUPI, 1999), http://www.dupi.dk/fmp4.0 /web/news. html#download.

C. de la Rey, 'Reconciliation in Divided Societies', D. Christie, et al. (eds), *Peace, Conflict and Violence* (Upper Saddle River: Prentice Hall, 2001), pp. 251-261.

J. Edelstein, 'Rights, Reparations and Reconciliation: Some Comparative Notes'. Paper presented at the Centre for the Study of Violence and Reconciliation, Seminar No. 6 (July 27, 1994), http://www.wits.ac.za/csvr/papedel. htm.

R. J. Fisher, 'Social-Psychological Processes in Interactive Conflict Analysis and Reconciliation' in Ho-Won Jeong (ed.), *Conflict Resolution: Dynamics, Process and Structure* (Aldershot: Ashgate, 1999).

J. Galtung, 'Peace and Conflict Research in the Age of the Cholera: Ten Pointers to the Future of Peace Studies'. *Peace and Conflict Studies*, vol. 4, no.1 (July 1995), http://www.trenton.edu/~psm/pcs/.

J. Galtung, 'After Violence: 3R, Reconstruction, Reconciliation, Resolution: Coping with Visible and Invisible Effects of War and Violence', *Transcend: A Peace and Development Network* (July 1998a), http://www.transcend.org/trrecbas. htm.

J. Galtung, *Conflict Transformation by Peaceful Means (The TRANSCEND Method): A Manual Prepared for the United Nations Disaster Management Training Program* (1998b), http://www.transcend.org/trmanpar. htm.

B. Hambler, 'Truth: The Road to Reconciliation?', *Cantilevers: Building Bridges for Peace*, vol. 3 (1998), http://sunsite.wits.ac.za/wits/csvr/artrcant.htm.

B. Hamber and H. van der Merwe, 'What Is this Thing Called Reconciliation'. Paper presented at the Goedgedacht Forum, *After the Truth and Reconciliation Commission*, Cape Town (March 28, 1998), http://www.wits.ac.za /csvr/artrcb&h.htm.

M. Henderson, *The Forgiveness Factor* (London: Grosvenor Books, 1996).

M. Ignatieff, 'Articles of Faith', *Index on Censorship* (May 1996), http://www.oneworld.org/index_oc/issue596/ ignatieff.html.

H. Kelman, 'The Interactive Problem-Solving Approach' in C. A. Crocker and F. O. Hampson, et al. (eds), *Managing Global Chaos: Sources of and Responses to International Conflict* (Washington D.C.: U.S. Institute of Peace, 1996).

H. C. Kelman, 'Social-Psychological Dimensions of International Conflict' in I. W. Zartman and J. L. Rasmussen (eds), *Peacemaking in International Conflict: Methods & Techniques* (Washington, D.C.: U.S. Institute of Peace, 1997).

R. O. Keohane, *After Hegemony: Cooperation and Discord in the World Political Economy* (Princeton: Princeton University Press, 1984).

L. Kriesberg, 'Coexistence and the Reconciliation of Communal Conflicts' in Eugene Weiner (ed.), *The Handbook of Interethnic Coexistence* (New York: The Continuum Publishing Company, 1998)

L. Kriesberg, 'Paths to Varieties of Intercommunal Reconciliation' in Ho-Won Jeong (ed.), *Conflict Resolution: Dynamics, Process and Structure.* (Aldershot: Ashgate, 1999).

J. E. Lane, *Politics and Society in Western Europe* (London: Sage, 1994).

J. P. Lederach, *Building Peace: Sustainable Reconciliation in Divided Societies* (Washington, D.C. : U.S. Institute of Peace, 1997).

C. O. Lerche, 'Truth Commissions and National Reconciliation: Some Reflections of Theory and Practice', *Peace and Conflict Studies*, vol. 7, no. 1 (June 2000).

I. Liebenberg and A. Zegeye, 'Pathway to Democracy? The Case of the South African Truth and Reconciliation Process'. *Social Identities*, vol. 4, no. 3 (1998), pp. 541-558.

M. Lumsden, 'Breaking the Cycle of Violence: Three Zones of Social Reconstruction' in H. Jeong (ed.), *Conflict Resolution: Dynamics, Process and Structure* (Aldershot: Ashgate, 1999).

W. Meninger, *The Process of Forgiveness* (New York: Continuum, 1996).

J. V. Montville, 'The Healing Function in Political Conflict Resolution' in D. Sandole and H. van der Merwe, *Conflict Resolution Theory and Practice: Integration and Application* (New York: Manchester University Press, 1993).

J. V. Montville, 'The Political Meaning of Traumatic Loss', *The Conflict Prevention Resource Site, Publications and Essays on Conflict Resolution and Related Fields* (1998a), http://www.crosslink.net/~wfwp/montville .htm.

J. V. Montville, 'Reconciliation as Realpolitik: Facing the Burdens of History in Political Conflict Resolution', *Unpublished Manuscript* (1998b).

T. P. Prado, 'Advocates and Guarantors: Establishing Participative Democracy in Post-War Guatemala', *Accord: An International Review of Peace Initiatives* (1998), http://www.c-r.org/cr/acc_guat/ prado.htm.

R. I. Rotberg and D. Thompson (eds), *Truth Versus Justice: The Morality of Truth Commissions* (Princeton: Princeton University Press, 2000).

G. Simpson, 'Reconstruction and Reconciliatoin: Emerging from Transition' in *Development in Practice*, vol. 7, no. 4 (1997), http://www.wits.ac.za/csvr/papr&rgs.htm.

H. van der Merwe, 'Relating Theory to the Practice of Conflict Resolution in South Africa' in D. Sandole and H. van der Merwe, *Conflict Resolution Theory and Practice: Integration and Application* (New York: Manchester University Press, 1993).

6   Gender in Post-Conflict Reconstruction

Susan McKay

Throughout the world, women's status is low when compared to that of men. The greater male control is within a society, the stronger is the patriarchal system so that political, economic and social institutions reflect this bias. Because men's status is greater than women's virtually everywhere in the world, women's power is diminished and their skills underutilised. The consequence is that societies do not develop fully because patriarchal priorities assert themselves and render women invisible. An aim of feminist gender analysis, therefore, is to make women's situations, perspectives and roles visible within these patriarchal contexts and their specific socio-political circumstances with the intent that this awareness will result in actions to change inequities. In conducting such analyses, the life conditions of both women and men are considered, that is -- 'how women and men are involved in society at different levels, what each contributes, their particular needs and interests, and how each gender benefits or suffers from policies and projects, including how resources and power are distributed and used' (Breines, 1999, p. 39).

GENDER ANALYSES

To help clarify how armed conflict, war-ending negotiations and peace accords, and post-conflict societal reconstruction processes are gendered to privilege men, feminist analysts make connections between war and other forms of political and personal violence, including in the post-conflict period when the violence of a war or political regimes often begets a general culture of violence (Enloe,

1993; Enloe, 2000; Mazurana & McKay, 1999; Turshen, 1998; Sorensen, 1998). They emphasise that women's peacebuilding actions are essential to help prevent war, end armed conflict and rebuild societies. Their analyses are instrumental in developing new insights about how peacebuilding may be distinctly construed by women and women's organizations, and stress that women must move from victim roles to become actors within the rebuilding of post-conflict societies at nongovernmental (NGO) and grassroots levels, where they readily forge a place for themselves (Mazurana & McKay, 1999).

In contrast to women's activities within NGOs and grassroots groups, women's increased participation in peacebuilding within public arenas does not happen easily because male dominance is pervasive. In response to this knowledge, international women's peacebuilding organisations and networks advocate that women must be 'at the table' where critical public discourse occurs and decisions are made (Anderlini, 2000). These groups believe that when women involve themselves in these public forums, their visions for peace, equality and social justice help societies to build a more secure future.

Gender-Based Violence, Intrastate Conflicts and Post-Conflict Peacebuilding

Conventional wars have, in the main, given way to intrastate conflicts which are legacies of colonialism, super-power rivalries and commercialism, and occur predominately within developing countries (Turpin, 1998; Turshen, 1998). At the heart of these intrastate armed conflicts are issues of gender, identity, ethnicity and/or religion, which frequently precipitate violence between neighbors, friends and relatives (Bennett, Bexley, & Warnock, 1995; International Alert, 2000). Contingent with the human costs of these conflicts is major destruction of civilian infrastructures -- such as roads, health facilities, crops and the environment -- resulting in effects such as malnutrition and inadequate access to health care (Levy & Sidel, 1995; McKay, 1998a; U.S. Agency for International Development [USAID], 2000). Civilians are estimated to comprise 85 to 95 percent of casualties, the majority of whom are women and children. Because of their unequal status, women are particularly vulnerable during attacks (USAID, 2000). In addition to physical injury, psychosocial effects occur because of forced displacement, torture, rape and witnessing killings, among other reasons (Sorensen, 1998; USAID, 2000). For example, in a study conducted in the aftermath of the war in Bosnia, women reported traumatic experiences of life-endangerment, loss of homes and properties, hunger and thirst, betrayal by neighbors, family and friends, physical illness and physical harm or injury -- including sexual violence and torture -- and they felt lonely, frightened, sad, bitter, lost and restless. Many had suicidal thoughts, and feelings of helplessness and hopelessness that were accompanied by anxiety, depression and isolation (Agger, 2000). In post-Apartheid South Africa, memories and trauma included physical, mental and collective effects (de la Rey & Owens, 1998). Consequently, many women's peacebuilding groups' initiatives focus upon community healing for women who have experienced these crimes (Machel, 2000). A common strategy of these groups is to combine community initiatives and indigenous healing practices to develop programs of psychosocial and community-based healing, often with particular attention to women's trauma (Agger, 2000; de la Rey, 2000; de la Rey & McKay, in press; McKay & de la Rey; 2001; Niens & Cairns, 2000; McKay, 1998a; McKay, 2000; Staub, 2000; Wessells & Monteiro, 2000).

Gender-Based Violence

In this chapter, I stress that because gender-based violence during and after armed conflict is so pervasive, it is a critical women's peacebuilding issue. Also, gender-based violence constitutes a formidable obstacle to women's ability to achieve equality, development and peace (United Nations [UN], 1996b). Gender-based violence means that violence is uniquely directed towards women and girls because of their gender. It takes place in homes, communities, displaced persons' camps and during flights to safety, and encompasses any act that is likely to or results in physical, sexual, and psychological harm or suffering. During the post-conflict period, gender-based violence continues but is most apt to occur within private spaces of homes and communities (USAID, 2000). Also, UN peacekeepers commonly perpetrate gender-based violence during the post-conflict period although these assaults are rarely reported or investigated (Ruecker, 2000). Particularly egregious forms of gender-based violence are systematic rape, sexual slavery and forced pregnancy -- with rape being the most pervasive form. A UN report commissioned by the Secretary-General of the impact of armed conflict on children (UN, 1996a), hereafter called the Graça Machel Study, explicates how rape is used as a deliberate weapon of war to humiliate and weaken the morale of the perceived enemy, terrorise populations and force the enemy to flee. For example, in Rwanda, rape and sexual mutilations were carried out with the aim of eradicating the Tutsi (Human Rights Watch/Africa, 1996). In East Timor, sexual violence by the Indonesian military and local militias occurred in the wake of the violence and destruction following East Timor's vote for independence from Indonesia. Women were abducted and some were taken into West Timor where they were raped daily and forced to perform household chores (Mydans, 2001).

Devastating effects of gender-based violence include sexually-transmitted diseases such as HIV/AIDS, damage to sexual and reproductive functions, humiliation, and anguish (Machel, 2000). Girls are especially vulnerable to rape because they are smaller, younger and often thought by their perpetrators to be less apt to be infected with HIV/AIDS or other sexually-transmitted diseases (McKay, 1998a). Another way girls are sexually traumatised is to be used as 'wives' of soldiers within armed forces (McKay & Mazurana, 2000).

Gender-based violence also causes psychological trauma in both victims and witnesses: 'The rape of one person is translated into an assault upon the community through the emphasis placed in every culture on women's sexual virtue: the shame of the rape humiliates the family and all those associated with the survivor' (Nowrojee & Ralph, 2000). The effects of rape can continue for years, decades and across generations. Families, communities and societies are all affected. An example is the occupation of Kuwait by the Iraqi military, when about two thousand Kuwaiti women were sexually assaulted. Rape victims were kept locked in the house, married victims were divorced and some rape victims were killed by men in their families (Tétreault, 1997).

Because of the frequency with which gender-based violence occurs during and after armed conflict, women's peacebuilding initiatives are crucially concerned with its physical, psychological, and social traumatic effects and seeking gender justice. Gender justice means 'legal processes which are equitable, not privileged by and for men, and which distinguish the nefarious forms of injustice women experience during and after armed conflict' (McKay, 2000, p. 561). Gender justice is affected by patriarchal privileges of post-conflict peacebuilding processes -- for example, courts reflect patriarchal bias so that when women's organisations and other advocacy groups seek justice in the face of gender-based violence, they seldom are successful. Therefore, international human rights, gender and feminist advocacy groups argue that gender-based violence during and after armed conflict must be recognised and advocated against, laws changed that currently protect perpetrators, and accountability and gender justice must occur in courts, war tribunals and other national and international venues. Given the great importance that redressing the effects of gender-based violence has for many local, national and international women's peacebuilding initiatives, examining mainstream meanings of peacebuilding can shed light upon whether these and related women's concerns are seen as 'the normal business of peacebuilding' or reflect patriarchal bias.

GENDERED MEANINGS OF PEACEBUILDING

Peacebuilding meanings vary within and among intergovernmental and governmental bodies, and other organisations such as NGOs. They influence defining interests of peacebuilding policies, processes and projects that are conceptualised and implemented (Mazurana & McKay, 1999). Some, but not many, meanings of peacebuilding take into account the critical importance of working towards equality, gender and social justice, promoting relational and consensual actions aimed at improving relationships, addressing basic needs and strengthening existing peace (for example, Fisher, 1993; Lederach 1995a; Lederach, 1995b). More commonly, as within Canadian foreign policy, peacebuilding highlights strengthening and solidifying peace by building a sustainable infrastructure of human security (Ruecker, 2000). Former UN Secretary General Boutros-Ghali's influential definition of peacebuilding, widely used as a blueprint for designing peacebuilding initiatives, emphasises construction of a new environment, support for transformation of deficient national structures and capabilities, and strengthening democratic institutions: 'action to identify and support structures which will tend to strengthen and solidify peace in order to avoid a relapse into conflict'. (Boutros-Ghali, 1992, p. 11). In contrast to the UN, governmental organisations and international NGOs' focus upon structural rebuilding; many grassroots women's groups and local NGOs call attention to gender concerns, psychosocial processes, and human needs and their critical influence in building sustainable peace (Mazurana & McKay, 1999; McKay & de la Rey, 2001).

Feminist Perspectives

What is notable about most peacebuilding meanings is that, outside of the work of grassroots' and women's peace groups, gender and gender concerns are invisible. Feminist examinations of meanings of post-conflict peacebuilding and its priorities, values and projects therefore give a perspective that contrasts with these mainstream definitions. Feminists observe that women's grassroots' and local NGOs' peacebuilding groups approach peacebuilding as an ongoing process that emphasises relationships, basic needs, nonviolence, forgiveness and reconciliation processes (de la Rey & McKay, in press; Mazurana & McKay, 1999; McKay & Mazurana, 2001; McKay & de la Rey, 2001). Also, they stress healing of psychological and spiritual wounds, promoting recovery from the past, and seeking gender and social justice (McKay, 2000). For example, in South Korea much of women's peacebuilding centres upon the pervasive militarism within the Korean peninsula and its effects upon women's lives, and in some cases, the relationship between past wartime rapes and present militarised recreational rapes (Enloe, 2000; McKay & Mazurana, 2001). Thus, some South

Korean women's peacebuilding NGOs are working in coalitions within the Asia-Pacific region to secure an official government apology from Japan and seek compensation for Korean and Filipino Comfort Women who were used by the Japanese military as sexual slaves during World War II.

Importantly, other women's peacebuilding groups focus upon reconciliation with North Korea, decreasing threats posed by nuclear arms and landmines, promoting human rights and gender equality, and advocating for increased democratisation (McKay & Mazurana, 2001). Activities in which these groups are involved include film production to highlight these issues, citizen exchanges between North and South Korea, and education about disarmament and alternative methods of conflict resolution. Protests, demonstrations and picketing are often used. Creative events such as art exhibitions, theatrical performances, film festivals and art forms are all instrumental in meeting peacebuilding goals. As is typical of most local women's grassroots groups and NGOs, they operate on tight budgets with limited financial support. Their work is context-specific because its emphasis is upon critical concerns for women's peacebuilding within the Korean peninsula, and it is informed by their own situation analyses (McKay & Mazurana, 2001).

As an outcome of a study of international women's peacebuilding and the meanings of peacebuilding at NGO and grassroots levels, Dyan Mazurana and I developed a feminist definition of peacebuilding that contrasts with commonly-used definitions:

> Peacebuilding includes gender-aware and women-empowering political, social, economic and human rights. It involves personal and group accountability and reconciliation processes which contribute to the reduction or prevention of violence. It fosters the ability of women, men, girls and boys in their own cultures to promote conditions of nonviolence, equality, justice and human rights of all people, to build democratic institutions and to sustain the environment (Mazurana & McKay, 1999, p. 9).

In a second study, we analysed women's use of media technologies in peacebuilding and concluded that issues women emphasise in their peacebuilding work is contextually specific and 'is shaped and influenced by the particular historical, social, economic, political and cultural factors of the country region, and conflict(s)', and these actions expand narrower definitions of peacebuilding (McKay & Mazurana, 2001, p. 75).

Gender activists use feminist analyses, such as ours, in their work to increase women's visibility and their political, economic and social involvement in peace negotiations and on the frontlines of reconstruction within post-conflict societies. They cite dual purposes of improving women's status and strengthening women's potential contributions to their country's long-term development, which may fare better because of their participation (USAID, 2000). Thus, within both public and private sectors, women's peacebuilding seeks greater equality for women. Important to note is that although statements upholding women's equality are included in constitutions within some newly-emerging democracies (for example, South Africa and Eritrea), in reality women's status rarely improves during the post-conflict period -- even if temporary change occurred when women assumed new roles and responsibilities during armed conflict. Therefore, effective women's peacebuilding insistently advocates for improving women's status. Also, these activists work to have gender-inclusive policies formulated within peace accords, national constitutions and in the restructuring of economic, social, political and legal systems. An example of these activities is Resolution 1325 that was adopted in October 2000 by the United Nations Security Council. This resolution calls for gender perspectives in negotiating and implementing peace agreements to include the special needs of women and girls during repatriation and resettlement, rehabilitation, reintegration and post-conflict reconstruction. Among its recommended measures are to support local women's peace initiatives and indigenous processes for conflict resolution, to involve women in implementing peace agreements and to ensure human rights of women and girls (UN, 2000).

GENDERED REALITIES IN POST-CONFLICT SOCIETIES

The overriding reality in post-conflict societies is that reconstruction processes privilege patriarchal institutions and processes. Cynthia Enloe observed that the war-ending process is profoundly gendered (1993). When societies restructure and rebuild, conflict invariably occurs between priorities of nationalism and progress towards women's equality. What usually happens is that nationalistic movements that advocate for women's equality retrench during the post conflict period and fail to fulfill these promises (Seidman, 1993, p. 291). Instead, women often are urged to return to traditional roles and domains of family and community, leaving men responsible for economic, political and social reconstruction (McKay, 1998b). Therefore, women wanting to shape the reconstruction of their countries are breaking with patriarchal tradition. With the formalisation of official peace negotiations and post-conflict rebuilding processes, women are usually excluded, because these are considered male domains, and they rapidly lose what influence they may have gained (Sorensen, 1998). The result is that peace negotiations and peacebuilding projects reflect male discourses and practices to the exclusion of women's priorities.

Those wanting to remain active as shapers of post-conflict societies battle against entrenched attitudes and powerful pressures, both social and economic, which advocate that they return to the domestic sphere (Bennett, Bexley & Warnock, 1995). In the process, they may be denied their human rights in health, education, and social services and marginalised from political processes, including access to decision-making positions (Ruecker, 2000). A USAID study concluded that women usually left public life when the hostilities stopped and identified a range of reasons. In some instances, the psychological stress of war generated nostalgia for returning to the traditional social and political order. In others, war fatigue contributed to women's decisions to leave public life. The most significant factor was that men sought to reassert their patriarchal authority once they were freed from preoccupation with war (USAID, 2000). Thus, strong societal sanctions may operate to discourage women's involvement in peacebuilding. In post-conflict

Guatemala, resistance to women's advocacy for gender equality occurred through public ridicule, harassment and violence in both private and public spheres. In Mozambique, women were urged to leave gender struggle behind (Urdang, 1989). Similarly, when Namibia gained independence from South Africa, the new constitution recognised women's special discrimination and called for affirmative action policies. Consistent with post-conflict gender reality, these women's hopes were ultimately disappointed (McKay, 1998b). Even when constitutions guarantee women's equal status in rebuilding societies, (as occurred in South Africa, Bosnia and Herzegovina, Cambodia and Guatemala), the reality is that these laws may not be implemented. Also, obstacles (such as lack of resources and gender awareness) influence the realisation of these goals (Sorensen, 1998; USAID, 2000).

Feminist Questions

Previously, I discussed how analysts use a gender perspective in attempt to make feminist sense of post-conflict realities. They seek to better understand how gender operates within post-conflict reconstruction and peacebuilding processes as well as ways patriarchal gender relations may be recreated. Questions they ask are, 'Where are the women, which women are there, how did those women get there and what do those women think about being there?' (Enloe, 2000, p. 294).

> What maneuverings does it take to position certain women in any society to support their governments in certain ways when those governments rank public priorities so that they bestow superior value on the military as an institution and on soldiering as a public activity? Among these feminist analysts' discoveries have been that governments and political leaders have invested a great deal of time and resources into shaping what it means to be a loyal wife, a patriotic mother, a modern woman, a professional nurse, a healthy prostitute, an ashamed rape victim, an understanding girlfriend...Decisions about women will...be made not just in the midst of that conflict, but in the years

preceding any anticipated conflict and in the years following that conflict (Enloe, 2000, p. 294).

Related questions follow: Who shapes post-conflict policies? Are women at the table negotiating peace accords to shape the post-conflict period? Why, despite women's expanded public roles during conflict, are they so often marginalised within post-conflict societies and urged to resume traditional roles within private spaces of home and family? In the aftermath of gender-based violence and other physical and psychosocial harm, what processes exist for women to seek and obtain justice? What emphasis is given to community building, healing relationships, and meeting people's basic needs? How do peace accords and legal systems -- including constitutions and processes of political participation -- reflect gender power relationships (McKay, 1998b)? How can a critical shift be made so that women become agents engaging in and using state processes for their own ends (Friedman, 2000)? Resulting analyses, although still incomplete in answering these complex questions, reveal patriarchal post-conflict reconstruction priorities and projects.

WOMEN BUILDING PEACE

Despite obstacles that arise from contending with patriarchal systems, women often are eager to contribute within their communities and countries in shaping post-conflict societies' futures. They often do so within grassroots groups and NGOs where they typically focus their peacebuilding work upon community-based peacebuilding initiatives that are context specific and process oriented (de la Rey & McKay, 2001; Mazurana & McKay, 1999; McKay & de la Rey, 2001; McKay & Mazurana, 2001). Critically important in their own right and capable of challenging authorities and members of civic society, these groups are often positioned outside the main corridors of power. Yet, they can achieve powerful results, and some of the women in these groups subsequently emerge as powerful players in national, regional and international arenas. Importantly, participating in these groups can provide new opportunities for women to try out unaccustomed roles as initiators and organisers of projects and programmes that build peace, seek justice and forge reconciliation between groups.

International Recognition

To increase the participation of women in peacebuilding, advocates urge governmental, intergovernmental and international organisations to involve women more fully. Consequently, women's peacebuilding is now recognised as crucially important at national, regional and international levels. An example of this acknowledgement was Resolution 1325 adopted by the UN Security Council in October 2000, mentioned previously. Also, the *Platform for Action* (*PFA*), an influential document accepted by international consensus at the UN Fourth World Conference on Women held in Beijing, China in 1995, explicates actions to be taken by international, regional, governmental and nongovernmental organisations and the private sector to empower women and encourage their increased involvement in peacebuilding (UN, 1986; McKay & Winter, 1998). Several of its key recommendations are relevant to women's peacebuilding: 'promote equal participation of women and equal opportunities for women to participate in all forums and peace activities at all levels, particularly at the decision-making level...' and to 'integrate a gender perspective in the resolution of armed or other conflicts and foreign occupation and aim for gender balance when nominating or promoting candidates for judicial and other positions in all international bodies' (UN, 1996b, pp. 85-86). Also, the Graça Machel Study (UN, 1996a) explicated the effects of armed conflict upon children, highlighted the critical nature of women's participation in stopping conflict and building peace—thereby linking children's situation with women's own: 'Women have been active agents of peacebuilding and conflict resolution at the local level and their participation at the national, regional and international levels should be increased' (UN, 1996a, p. 75). These international documents draw attention to the critical importance of women's peacebuilding actions and advocate for women's empowerment as actors in post-conflict societies, especially within their own communities.

Peacebuilding Actions and Strategies

Elise Boulding noted that because, in the existing social order, women are usually marginal in public decision-making, they are freer to act because they have fewer vested interests to protect (2000). Thus, their peacebuilding may use unique strategies that Boulding calls 'women's inventions'. NGOs and grassroots groups may involve themselves in nonviolent actions -- in creative ways such as dressing in black, employing street theatre, holding vigils and demonstrations, and organising peace camps and peace walks. Such actions can be dangerous when these groups demand accountability, an end of violence, and promotion of peace and protest when other groups do not dare (Mazurana & McKay, 1999). Regardless of the form of their peacebuilding, their involvement:

> enhances the legitimacy of the process by making it more democratic and responsive to the priorities of all sectors of the affected population. Their absence from this process results in setbacks to the development of society at large, undermines democracy, and affects women's political participation, economic security and social development in terms of gaining rights and equality (Anderlini, 2000, pp 5-6).

A common peacebuilding strategy is for women to form networks and coalitions where they meet to plan, gain energy and push for peace regionally and globally, or show that peace is possible between conflicting groups (Mazurana & McKay, 1999). Thus, in Lebanon, local NGOs used networks linked with international NGOs and UN representatives to strengthen global networks and local women's peacebuilding initiatives. These NGOs reinforced civil society by increasing citizen awareness, defending civilian rights and acting as a vigilant body (Mazurana & McKay, 1999). In Guatemala,

> women organised early in the peace process and because of effective lobbying, were able to create a 'women's sector' to provide feedback to the government. The women's

sector, originally a very divided cross section of 45 women's groups, emerged, after hard work and negotiations, within two weeks, as an effective local NGO lobbying group for women. Encompassing 94 groups by 1997, the sector has worked to influence implementation of the peace accords. Throughout their work, members of the women's sector learned hands-on democratic processes and nonviolent conflict management and resolution (Manning & Arneil as cited in Mazurana & McKay, 1999, p. 42).

Seeking Gender Justice

Peacebuilding, as presently understood, seldom incorporates concern for gender-based violence or initiatives to achieve gender justice. As I have argued, women's peacebuilding groups often view gender-based violence to be a central issue and as necessary to accomplish in moving closer to creating more equitable, just and democratic societies. These groups reason that effective societal peacebuilding must include a commitment to gender justice because recovery from war trauma requires that people come to terms with atrocities as a prelude to effective peacebuilding. Therefore, many women's NGOs and grassroots peacebuilding groups advocate against impunity and for gender justice. A critical debate has arisen between secular and religious groups about whether reconciliation and effective post-conflict peacebuilding are possible in the absence of gender justice.

Religious and ethnic groups often emphasise forgiveness. Seeking gender justice may be viewed as subordinate or even damaging, and can be an impediment to redressing past wrongs. This reasoning relates to a spiritual belief that changing the heart (forgiveness, love, charity) is more critical than changing the mind (legal justice). Similarly, religious and spiritual traditions may urge women to forgive and forget gender-specific violence. This stance can reinforce impunity because perpetrators are never punished for their crimes (McKay, 2000). A related perspective arises from some cultural traditions. When ethnic communities with long histories of intermarriage engage in armed conflicts, truth-telling in the aftermath and a quest for gender justice may reactivate inter-tribal conflicts. Thus silence about gender-specific violence may be viewed as necessary for communities to reconcile and build peace (Lydia Ajono, personal communication, November 1999). Although recognising these important religious and cultural perspectives, most women's peacebuilding groups that work for gender justice believe it pre-eminent over processes of forgiveness and reconciliation. Truth-telling and gender justice are consequently considered to be prerequisites to reconciliation and effective peacebuilding (McKay, 2000). Because a major difficulty in significant progress towards achieving gender justice is judicial bias and women's lack of power in obtaining justice, gender advocacy groups often support women in telling their stories within national and international fora and truth commissions and in seeking restitution. They ask for legal prosecution within these bodies and organise class action suits to sue perpetrators to compel the responsible State to compensate survivors.

Examples illustrate how several women's peacebuilding groups have pressed for gender justice. In South Africa, women's groups saw to it that gender issues were placed on the agenda of the Truth and Reconciliation Commission (TRC). They also made recommendations to improve women's participation in the TRC process. The result was that women's voices were heard in the emerging history that the Commission shaped (Goldblatt & Meintjes, 1998). In East Timor, a leading women's aid organisation researched and documented gender-based violations to be used in forthcoming war tribunal trials (Mydans, 2001). Also, international women's actions for gender justice were crucial in the February 2001 decision at the International Criminal Tribunal for the Former Yugoslavia when two Bosnian Serbs were convicted of crimes against humanity because of rape. This was the first time sexual slavery has been prosecuted and condemned by an international tribunal and rape ruled as a crime against humanity. These rulings occurred in large part because international women's peacebuilding groups pressed the Tribunal to prosecute sexual violence as war crimes (Simons, 2001). Despite these important precedents, gender justice is still out of reach for most women and few perpetrators are punished (Amadiume & An-Na'im, 2000). The result is that gender justice remains elusive, especially with respect to gender-based violence, and remains a central concern of women's peacebuilding.

CONCLUSION

Women's peacebuilding actions promote gender-aware and women-empowering political, social, economic and human rights. They seek to reduce the incidence of gender-based violence and other physical and psychological harm that occurs during and after armed conflict, assure that women's perspectives are made visible and improve women's status within post-conflict societies. Because women are usually marginalised within post-conflict societies, women's grassroots groups and NGOs have become influential in bringing their peacebuilding concerns to the forefront and creatively using their energies to forge change. Through these groups, many women become involved in peacebuilding and, in the process, increase their own capacities as actors within their communities, countries and regions. Through their involvement, they provide critical national and international leadership and promote conditions of nonviolence, equality, justice and human rights. Also, they emphasise human processes -- including the achievement of personal and group accountability and reconciliation processes -- that contribute to the reduction or prevention of violence. A critical peacebuilding issue that is a focus for many of these groups is that gender-based violence, whether within public or private spaces and during or after armed conflict, must be acknowledged and gender justice sought.

Because of the important contributions of women, post-conflict peacebuilding must involve them as essential actors and societies should examine peacebuilding processes to determine whether they privilege patriarchal priorities and projects through the existing paradigms. Unfortunately, in the present international context, post-conflict societies have yet to take full advantage of women's peacebuilding contributions and the visions they promote -- because to do so threatens patriarchal institutions and privileges.

I wish to thank Dyan Mazurana for her careful review of the first draft of this chapter.

REFERENCES

I. Agger, 'Reducing Trauma during Ethno-Political Conflict: A Personal Account of Psycho-Social Work under War Conditions in Bosnia', in D. Christie, R. Wagner and D. DuNann Winter (eds), *Peace, Conflict, and Violence: Peace Psychology for the 21st Century* (Upper Saddle River: Prentice Hall, 2000), pp. 240-250.

I. Amadiume and A. An-Na'im, *The Politics of Memory: Truth, Healing and Social Justice* (London: Zed Books, 2000).

S. Anderlini, *Women at the Peace Table: Making a Difference* (New York: United National Development Fund for Women, 2000).

O. Bennett, J. Bexley and K. Warnock, *Arms to Fight, Arms to Protect* (London: Panos Publications, Ltd., 1995).

E. Boulding, *Cultures of Peace: The Hidden Side of History* (Syracuse: Syracuse University Press, 2000).

B. Boutros-Ghali, *An Agenda for Peace: Preventive Diplomacy, Peacemaking, and Peace-keeping* (New York: United Nations, 1992).

I. Breines, 'A Gender Perspective on a Culture of Peace', in I. Breines, D. Gierycz and B. Reardon (eds), *Towards a Women's Agenda for a Culture of Peace* (Paris: United Nations Education, Scientific, and Cultural Organisation Publishing, 2000), pp. 33-56.

C. de la Rey, 'Reconciliation in Divided Societies', in D. Christie, R. Wagner and D. DuNann Winter (eds), *Peace, Conflict, and Violence: Peace Psychology for the 21ˢᵗ Century* (Upper Saddle River: Prentice Hall, 2000), pp. 251-261.

C. de la Rey and S. McKay, 'Peace as a Gendered Process: Perspectives of Women Doing Peacebuilding in South Africa', *Peace and Conflict Studies* (In Press).

C. de la Rey, and I. Owens, 'Perceptions of Psychosocial Healing and the Truth and Reconciliation Commission in South Africa', *Peace and Conflict: Journal of Peace Psychology*, vol. 4 (1998), pp. 257-270.

C. Enloe, *Maneuvers: The International Politics of Militarizing Women's Lives* (Berkeley: University of California Press, 2000).

C. Enloe, *The Morning After: Sexual Politics at the End of the Cold War* (Berkeley: University of California Press, 1993).

R. Fisher, 'The Potential for Peacebuilding: Forging a Bridge from Peacekeeping to Peacemaking', *Peace and Change*, vol. 18 (1993), pp. 247-266.

M. Friedman, 'Effecting Equality: Translating Commitment into Policy and Practice', *Agenda*, vol. 42 (2000), pp. 1-17.

B. Goldblatt and S. Meintjes, 'South Africa Women Demand the Truth', in M. Turshen and C. Twagiramariya (eds), *What Women Do in Wartime* (London: Zed Books, 1998), pp. 27-61.

Human Rights Watch/Africa, *Shattered Lives: Sexual Violence during the Rwandan Genocide and Its Aftermath* (New York: Human Rights Watch, 1996).

International Alert, *Women, Conflict, and Peacebuilding, a Preliminary Audit: The Beijing Platform for Action, Achievements and Emerging Challenges* (London: International Alert, 2000).

J. P. Lederach, *Building Peace: Sustainable Reconciliation in Divided Societies* (Tokyo: United Nations University, 1995a).

J. P. Lederach, *Preparing for Peace* (Syracuse: Syracuse University Press, 1995b).

B. Levy and V. Sidel (eds), *War and Public Health* (New York: Oxford University Press, 1996).

G. Machel, 'The Machel Review Document, The Impact of Armed Conflict on Children: Four Years Later', Paper prepared for the International Conference on War-Affected Children (Winnipeg: September 2000).

D. Mazurana and S. McKay, *Women and Peacebuilding* (Montreal: International Centre for Human Rights and Democratic Development, 1999).

S. McKay, 'Gender Justice and Reconciliation', *Women's Studies International Forum*, vol. 25, no. 5 (2000), pp. 1-10.

S. McKay, 'The Effects of Armed Conflict on Girls and Women,' *Peace and Conflict: Journal of Peace Psychology*, vol. 4 (1998a), pp. 381-392.

S. McKay, 'The Psychology of Societal Reconstruction and Peace: A Gendered Perspective', in L. Lorentzen and J. Turpin (eds), *The Women and War Reader* (New York: New York University Press, 1998b), pp. 348-362.

S. McKay and C. de la Rey, 'Women's Meanings of Peacebuilding in Post-Apartheid South Africa', *Peace and Conflict: Journal of Peace Psychology*, vol. 7 (2001), pp. 227-242.

S. McKay and D. Mazurana, 'Girls in Militaries, Paramilitaries and Armed Opposition Groups,' Paper prepared for the International Conference on War-Affected Children (Winnipeg: September 2000).

S. McKay and D. Mazurana, *Raising Women's Voices for Peacebuilding: Vision, Impact and Limitations of Media Technologies* (London: International Alert, 2001).

S. McKay and D.Winter, 'The United Nations' Platform for Action: Critique and Implications', *Peace and Conflict: Journal of Peace Psychology*, vol. 4 (1998), pp. 167-178.

S. Mydans, 'Sexual Violence as Tool of War: Pattern Emerging in East Timor', *New York Times*, CL (51,679) (01 March 2001), 1A.

U. Niens and E. Cairns, 'Intrastate Violence', in D. Christie, R. Wagner and D. DuNann Winter (eds), *Peace, Conflict, and Violence: Peace Psychology for the 21st Century* (Upper Saddle River: Prentice Hall, 2000), pp. 39-48.

B. Nowrojee and R. Ralph, 'Justice for Women Victims of Violence: Rwanda after the 1994 Genocide', in I. Amadiume and A. An-Na'im (eds), *The Politics of Memory: Truth, Healing and Social Justice* (London: Zed Books, 2000), pp. 162-175.

K. Ruecker, *Engendering Peacebuilding: Case Studies from Cambodia, Rwanda, and Guatemala* (Ottawa: Peacebuilding and Human Security Division, Department of Foreign Affairs and International Trade, 2000).

G. Seidman, 'No Freedom without the Women: Mobilization and Gender in South Africa, 1970-1992', *Signs: Journal of Women in Culture and Society*, vol. 18 (1993), pp. 291-320.

M. Simons, '3 Serbs Convicted in Wartime Rape', *New York Times, CL* (51,673) (February 23, 2001), 1A.

B. Sorensen, *Women and Post-Conflict Reconstruction: Issues and Sources* (Geneva: United Nations Research Institute for Social Development, 1998).

E. Staub, 'Genocide and Mass Killing: Their Roots and Prevention', in D. Christie, R. Wagner and D. DuNann Winter (eds), *Peace, Conflict, and Violence: Peace Psychology for the 21ˢᵗ Century* (Upper Saddle River: Prentice Hall, 2000), pp. 76-86.

M. A. Tétreault, 'Justice for All: Wartime Rape and Women's Human Rights', *Global Governance*, vol. 3 (1997), pp. 197-212.

J. Turpin, 'Many Faces: Women Confronting War', in L. Lorentzen and J.Turpin (eds), *The Women and War Reader* (New York: New York University Press, 1998), pp. 3-18.

M. Turshen, 'Women's War Stories', in M. Turshen and C. Twagiramariya (eds), *What Women Do in Wartime* (London: Zed Books, 1998), pp. 1-26.

United Nations, *Impact of Armed Conflict on Children: Report of the Expert of the Secretary-General Ms. Graça Machel* (New York: United Nations, 1996a).

United Nations, *The Beijing Declaration and the Platform for Action* (New York: United Nations, 1996b).

United Nations, 'Security Council Unanimously Adopting Resolution 1325 Calls for Broad Participation of Women in Peace-building, Post-conflict Reconstruction' (31 October 2000), http://www.un.org.

S. Urdang. *And Still They Dance: Women, War and the Struggle for Change in Mozambique* (New York: Monthly Review Press, 1989).

United States Agency for International Development, *Women and Women's Organisations in Post-Conflict Societies: The Role of International Assistance,* USAID Program and Operations Assessment Report no. 28 (Washington, D.C.: USAID, December 2000).

M. Wessells and C. Monteiro, 'Psychosocial Intervention and Post-War Reconstruction in Angola: Interweaving Western and Traditional Approaches', in D. Christie, R. Wagner and D. DuNann Winter (eds), *Peace, Conflict, and Violence: Peace Psychology for the 21ˢᵗ Century* (Upper Saddle River: Prentice Hall, 2000), pp. 262-275.

Part IV: Policy Design and Operational Issues

7 Peacebuilding Design: A Synergetic Approach

Ho-Won Jeong

The demand for more systematic approaches to peacebuilding persists due to scattered efforts made in rebuilding post-conflict societies. Too many projects end up being unsustainable because of the absence of both compelling goals for peace and co-ordinated strategies to achieve them. The recent practice of peacebuilding following the settlement of serious violent conflicts has largely been an institutional and operational adjustment of peacekeeping and humanitarian intervention.

It is important to develop a clear understanding of the diverse dimensions of peacebuilding and how various strategies can be put together to achieve sustainable peace. Therefore, a peacebuilding design process has to be more than a checklist of a vast array of tasks such as demobilisation, disarmament and institutional reform. In this chapter, a synergetic model is suggested for a more concerted approach to rebuilding post-conflict societies.

DESIGN PRINCIPLES

Peacebuilding design should not simply be an exercise for developing inventories of measurable outputs, but has to help clarify priorities of goals, identify the means to achieve them and assess their effects on the overall process. While the goals have to be defined in terms of desirable conditions for peace, implementation strategies need to focus on the identification of actors, co-ordination of activities and establishment of a time frame (whether short-term or long-term). A strategy also needs to be understood in terms of the way available tools can be deployed in the pursuit of goals (Kraybill, 2001; Magolin and Buchanan, 1998).

Policy frameworks and planning have to consider the analysis of not only the scope and duration of the impact of any policy options but also their opportunity costs as related to the level of sustained efforts required for the achievement of policy objectives. In assessing strategies, therefore, the possible effect of policy alternatives and its salience can be compared with the time needed to achieve policy goals and degrees of difficulties for policy implementation. Sustainability can be incorporated into strategic analysis, since no matter how ideal the outcome might be, it has to be durable in terms of creating the necessary infrastructure for long-term peace as well as being achievable within an acceptable time frame.

Multi-dimensional analysis helps assess the strengths of the peace potential by examining the impact of diverse policy tools on the outcome (Lund, 2001). The design for a peace structure has to be able to identify peacebuilding blocs, which impact social, psychological, political and economic dimensions of a peace process. A coherent policy plan has to consider mutual effects of a series of both direct and indirect measures, which either accelerate or inhibit progress toward the implementation of a peace agreement.

Designing a conceptual model for a system-wide strategic plan has to be supported by a comprehensive analysis of the original conflict. Different components of peacebuilding have to consider a diverse nature of past violence and its causal antecedents as well as an assessment of future developments. The memories of past events and visions for the future all have an impact on the present struggle.

Whereas generic categories of peacebuilding can be listed in an inclusive design (Doyle and Sambanis, 2000), a standard model has to be adapted to developing strategies responding to specific sets of problems. The 'very notion of peace is understood as social constructions shaped by a particular material and political context' (Lizee, 1999, p. 18). The different needs faced by societies recovering from a violent political conflict (for instance, a civil war in El Salvador, Guatemala, Mozambique, Cambodia and Liberia) have to be incorporated in a peacebuilding design.

Since peacebuilding processes are not necessarily the same, contextual variables are important for policy implementation. The comparative analysis of South Africa, Bosnia and Rwanda suggests that the level of violence (civil war versus limited armed struggle) and the methods for ending violent conflict (negotiated settlement versus military victory) have an impact on post-conflict political dynamics. Longer and more complex processes are needed for societies emerging from ethnic cleansing or deep political rivalries (for example, Bosnia and Somalia) to recover. Ending conflict with military victory creates unbalanced power relations that in turn lead to difficulties in democratic governance as were exemplified by Rwanda and the Democratic Republic of Congo.

A peace process can be beset by the fractured and divided nature of groups and a weak political and administrative infrastructure. The extent of economic and social destruction as well as the degree of ethnic rivalries has an impact on the rehabilitation and reconciliation process. More serious political and social challenges have to be overcome in rebuilding such societies as the Balkans, which have multiple ethnic groups, a collapsed economy, radical changes in ethnic boundaries and the malfunction of the central government.

DEFINING GOALS AND STRATEGIES

Sustainable peace can be defined as a collective good to overcome the past legacy of violent conflict, underscoring the importance of helping the population effectively challenge extreme vulnerability to achieve self-sufficiency. Thus the goal of peacebuilding would be reduction not only in physical and material sufferings but also in organisational and social vulnerabilities along with attitudinal and motivational changes needed in the deconstruction of a violence system. Integrative social development, based on human needs, should be the ultimate focus of post-conflict reconstruction and rehabilitation.

The process of post-conflict peacebuilding is characterised by a move from the reality of violence and domination to the creation of conditions for lasting peace (Franck, 1998; Lumsden, 1999). More specifically, peacebuilding 'is composed of sequential activities with a series of interconnected movements in various sectors leading from vulnerability to well-being' (Leychler, 2000a, p. 1). In strengthening processes and structures to prevent violent conflict, reconstruction has to intersect with relief and development activities (Goodhand and Hulme, 1997). Long-term development agendas are needed for substantive achievement in reconstituting war-torn societies while short-term relief is provided by humanitarian assistance.

Formal agreements at a political level focus on arms reduction, restoration of law and order and liberal economic reform, while community level activities are concerned about everyday violence against women, children and minority group members. Strategies at a national level cannot be effective without the support of grassroots projects, which improve social and economic life. Institutionalisation of peacebuilding has to be balanced with creative processes existing at a local level.

Sustainable peacebuilding is primarily the task of former adversaries supported by external assistance (Cockell, 2000). A social process for an associative engagement should integrate multifaceted peacebuilding dimensions. The overall aim is to create a mutually beneficial sense of interdependence among all the parties and to embed stable relations into institutions. The anarchic relationship between former belligerents must be substituted with a mutually accepted framework of rules and institutions guiding their conduct (Pugh, 2000).

If one of the parties is not serious about implementing the peace agreements and violates rules, difficult policy questions arise. Obviously, political decisions involve a balance between dealing with obstructers and identifying supportive elements. Policy tools and mechanisms have to be developed for weakening those spoilers who attempt to disrupt a peace process. Adopting appeasement strategies without specific principles has not proven productive; it involves the issues of fairness and encourages further demands of the obstructive party. In fact, the case of Cambodia suggests that concessions to an aggressive faction can bring about a more disruptive result. On the other hand, the application of successful coercion has not been easy without well co-ordinated efforts, as we have seen in the failure of arresting a warlord in Somalia and controlling national extremists in Bosnia.

Coercive measures involve a lot of risks, and their effects on the targeted groups may not be easily observed without high costs. Coercion is a short-term option, and has to be used in the context to prevent recurrent violence (Stedman and Rothchild, 1997). Enforcement options can be balanced by political compromise sought through negotiations. The choice of sanctions or negotiated compromise depends on their impact on the overall peacebuilding structure. While the amendment to previous agreements may be possible, faced with the need for adjustment to the new situation, the parties have to re-confirm their commitment to the peace process.

Effective communication between former enemies is essential for confidence building. This can be achieved through an effective operation of such mechanisms as a joint political military commission in Mozambique. Various national forums were organised in South Africa and Ethiopia to discuss a nation building process. Institutions that facilitate a collaborative process can help reduce transaction costs in managing relationships between various parties. The identification of common interests through negotiation, consultation, mediation and problem solving measures contributes to sustaining and reinforcing the process to explore mutually satisfying formulas (Fisher, 1999). The system of communication also has to allow the expression of unmet interests for marginalised groups and translation of their concerns into constructive agendas.

Exogenous Support and Endogenous Initiatives

In contrast with exogenous measures, which depend on initiatives prescribed, induced or imposed externally or from the top, endogenous measures are elicited from those directly affected by the outcome. A long-term process of socio-economic transformation can be best sustained by groups within a society through indigenous approaches. The assessment of the indigenous capabilities of local communities and their needs can be made in a way to identify the areas requiring external support. The success or failure of peacebuilding is affected by internal dynamics as well as external influence. Some conflicts can be transformed by the evolution of intra-communal relationships (Jeong, 2000), while in other situations, the opportunity can be provided by external actors. The role of external support has to be flexibly adapted to a specific conflict context (Thayer, 1998). The extent of external involvement in reconstruction depends on the degree of local administrative capacity as well as the level of collaborative spirits between former adversaries. External intervention should help the creation of a mutually interdependent relationship and reduction in asymmetric economic and political power.

The nature of intervention is related to the level of commitment of major political forces to a peace process and the existing level of trust between them (Maynard, 1997). In Namibia, short-term objectives of demilitarisation were a main focus since they were considered important for the promotion of political stability. Due to the willingness of major antagonists to abide by the agreed rules, the implementation of demobilisation and disarmament of combatants in Namibia did not invite significant external intervention, compared with the Mozambique case in which external pressure was critical in gaining compliance from rebel forces. With the existence of suspicion and ambivalence, external support and pressure were used to provide assurances and increase the stakes so that the rebel forces would not withdraw from the election process.

In the absence of an internally sustainable support structure, foreign assistance can strengthen the components that are essential for durable peace. Its significance is well illustrated by the fact that the incapacity and unwillingness of the international community to commit enough resources can weaken the peace implementation process as in the case of Angola where the parties lacked a collaborative mechanism. Its failed peace process is contrasted with a more successful example of Mozambique, which was strongly supported by the UN leadership (Anstee, 1996). A lack of sufficient support for the Angola operation is, in part, directly related to competition for resources with Cambodia, El Salvador and Mozambique (Malaquias, 1997).

Peacebuilding has to raise hope for integrative social development with the mobilisation of people's long-term commitment to a shared future and improvement of indigenous capacity. Thus, one of the most critical conditions to make a peace process sustainable is the engagement of local communities. The question of ownership of the process by broad sectors of society is a key to the effectiveness of the participatory mechanisms upon which the implementation of the accords depends.

Capacity of internal actors has to increase with reduction in international assistance. Political legitimacy can be based on external norms but has to be supported by local reality. Such terms as 'accountability' and 'good governance' have been interpreted in terms of a Western normative order, and have been applied without considering strategies, which are more suitable for local cultures and social structures. Indigenous economic and social programmes have to be strengthened to satisfy the local community's needs.

The Scope of Changes

Each peacebuilding measure differs in terms of the width and depth of its impact on the overall process. The scope of changes is affected by orientations of different peace approaches. Some measures concentrate on law and order with an emphasis on the restoration of a strong government while others are more geared toward facilitating a change in the existing social structures associated with a violent political order. In order to broaden the impact of democratisation, rebuilding local institutions has to be linked to civil society building.

The maintenance of cease-fires, humanitarian relief and the conduct of elections constitute a formal peacebuilding package (UN Department for Economic and Social Information and Policy Analysis, 1996). The majority of international programmes focus on the creation of institutions for the rule of law but evade their substantive content (Mani, 2000). In a minimalist approach, whose primary goal is to keep order, peacebuilding is considered only in a context of controlling a volatile situation without necessarily creating positive conditions for structural transformation. If political reform is not supported by nurturing civil society, the social-political dimension of peacebuilding is highly fragmented. Non-state associations can embody the elements of trust, cooperation and inclusion for the growth of mature civil society (Bernardo and Ortigas, 2000). The example of Liberia's election of a former warlord as president suggests that formal elections not accompanied by grassroots empowerment could end up strengthening centrifugal forces and allowing political oppression. In El Salvador and Guatemala, the political elites who were responsible for atrocities during the civil wars remained in office, and the continued domination of the military and landlords weakened the prospect for democracy and economic reform (Holiday and Stanley, 2000; Jonas, 2000; Popkin, 2000). Despite international assistance and internal demands, the El Salvadoran government resisted the legal and economic reform for land redistribution. The government also used insecurity and rising crime rates as excuses for delaying police reform (Cana and Dada, 1999).

Stable political order does not necessarily emerge from a new constitutional framework. Political mobilisation in a divided society often leads to strengthening ethno-nationalism and politics of exclusion and partisan loyalties (Byrne and Keashly, 2000). In an ethnically divided situation, opposing values and norms hamper the application of competitive, pluralistic, Western democratic principles.

Democracy can be consolidated with mature political conditions promoting both external and internal legitimacy (Silver, 1999; Wood, 2000). However, many new governments established by Western assistance do not meet those criteria. Hunsen's government in Cambodia violently eliminated opposition party members from the coalition government, which was created by a power-sharing arrangement following their defeat in the national election. A vacuum of political will and authority in Haiti hampered social stability and did not improve economic situations.

Peace stands in tension with the dynamics emerging from the tendency of political forces and social structures to reproduce violence over time. Thus the nature of peace prevailing in society is determined by the extent to which coercion and violence are delegitimised for reproduction of political order. Peacebuilding is affected by specific configurations of social structures and political forces. A particular structure (sustained by the maintenance of social cleavages in ethnicity, religion and language as well as concentration of economic wealth) fashions a social discourse legitimising the existing political order and violence, which in turn further perpetuates disparities among groups.

Transforming the existing social, economic and political structures is not achieved by a 'quick-fix' engineering approach since a wider and greater impact on the system can be brought about only by structural changes (Pugh, 2000). Overcoming the structural, cultural and relational roots underlying conflicts requires the transformation of root causes rather than re-establishing formal legal and institutional processes (Montiel, 2001).

In terms of the scope of changes, projects can focus either on improving individual well being or on institutional reform. The initial priority can be placed on improving inter-group relations prior to structural reform. Practical conflict resolution skills (applied to changes in attitudes, perceptions and behaviour) can have more impact on individual and group levels than broad social relations. Training programmes for inter-personal reconciliation can bring about intensive psychological effects at a small group level (Kelman, 1998). Compared with reconciliation programmes, development assistance affects more people, but generally has a less intensive impact on inter-personal processes.

In order to contribute to changes in conflict dynamics, approaches oriented toward individual needs or inter-personal issues have to broaden the base by moving beyond a small number of beneficiaries. Reconstruction programmes have to pay attention to reducing social discrimination as well as to improving social welfare conditions for underprivileged groups. The active engagement of a small group of people can be expanded to reach reform in social hierarchies through community building projects. Involving more individuals for institutional reform can broaden the base of grassroots projects. A wider and greater change derives from expanding a tangible impact at the lowest grassroots level.

A SYNERGETIC MODEL

Peacebuilding efforts can generate a synergetic impact by simultaneously stimulating the fulfillment of various requirements. In the synergetic interaction, the total effect is greater than the sum of the individual effects. In the design of a coherent action plan for building sustainable peace, any measures have to be considered in terms of complex interdependencies across domains (political, military, humanitarian, social and economic), time frames (long-term or short-term) and levels (intra- and inter-community).

Domains

The complexities of peacebuilding require coherent approaches to the multiple domains of peacebuilding, including disarmament, development, human rights and political reform. Activities in one policy sector can have either a positive or negative impact on other sectors. When they are not integrated in a complementary manner, uni-dimensional measures can have undesirable effects in other arenas, and even well intended measures can entail negative effects. The positive impact should be strong enough to reduce the negative externalities.

Multi-tasks of peacebuilding are faced with overcoming humanitarian sufferings and economic destruction as well as institutional failure. Humanitarian responses have a great impact on the overall peacebuilding process by facilitating social rehabilitation with the protection of minority ethnic groups exposed to violence. In particular, great attention needs to be paid to communities where the returning populations displaced by armed conflict have to be re-integrated into a new communal relationship for rebuilding a social and economic infrastructure.

The maintenance of cease-fires, humanitarian relief and successful completion of elections are necessary but are not themselves sufficient conditions for generating long-term synergetic effects. Less attention has been paid to qualitative social development than emergency activities. Obviously an adequate level of controlling physical violence and maintaining order is a precondition for economic and social development as well as institution building. However, disarmament and demobilisation alone cannot eliminate the danger of re-escalation. Enforcing negative peace, without social and economic development, is a slippery slope towards the inadvertent return to the origin of problems.

Integrated social development has a synergetic impact on the control of social violence. In the absence of recovery of economic activities and affirmation of human rights, as examples of El Salvador, Guatemala, Haiti and South Africa suggest, there is an increasing risk of getting caught up in criminal and socio-political violence. Development and social rehabilitation strategies have to be designed in a way that reduces a high level of crime, insecurity and volatile socio-political situations following the demobilisation of soldiers.

Capacity building is essential to the empowerment of local communities beyond the realisation of the immediate survival of those communities. The gap between humanitarian aid and reconstruction programmes hampers integrative approaches to community building. Development funding has to increase with a reduced role of emergency and other humanitarian intervention. With careful phasing out of humanitarian and emergency relief, investment for long-term development is directed toward overcoming poverty, income gaps, rising gender inequalities, educational decline and unemployment. Development measures have a more synergetic impact than military intervention by satisfying long-term requirements of social rehabilitation.

Reconstruction (supported by micro-credit programmes, revitalisation of small holder agriculture and improved access to land and credit) contributes more to the control of greater propensity for violent conflict by promoting equitable development. On the other hand, a focus on market dependent growth strategies fails to mitigate income gaps between social groups with different skills and resources (Harris, 1999). Economic liberalisation and privatisation can have negative effects on communal harmony and security with an unbalanced growth. Economic development and democratisation have a synergetic impact on each other. In a society with growing income gaps, economic privatisation produces a negative synergy for political democratisation. On the other hand, democratisation is supported by the achievement of a high level of socio-economic welfare.

Since democracy and development cannot be separately pursued due to their interdependent nature, measures, which are designed to advance the projected goals of democratisation and development, have to be compatible with each other. Sustainable social and economic development contributes to community building at a local level and a positive democratic environment at a national level by promoting even development of different segments of society. In particular, development is not dissociated from a democratisation process, which permits grassroots activities for the moblisation of resources.

Time Frames

In implementing a multi-phase programme, multi-component strategies can be combined either in terms of a sequential or synchronic order. The implementation of peacebuilding has been considered largely in terms of a sequential order, which suggests different time frames for crisis management, institution building and structural transformation. There are different circumstances under which short-, middle- and long-term programmes can be effectively implemented (Miall, et al., 1999). The goals of short-term military and diplomatic approaches are to avert violence and manage crisis while long-term approaches focus on changing social and economic conditions underpinning conflict.

At an early post-conflict stage, stability depends on the control of both an intensive and extensive level of violence (Walter, 1999). Many projects related to humanitarian aid and peacekeeping mostly deal with immediate concerns of human well being. Dispute resolution programmes such as mediation, conciliation and arbitration can be introduced to diffuse tensions arising from contradictory claims over properties and land (Jett, 1999). Short-term projects of conflict management have to proceed to long-term structural reform. Land re-distribution, community development programmes and commitment to democratic rule are critical to a long-term stability. Whereas elections and the re-establishment of formal political institutions can immediately follow the control of military violence, social and economic reconstruction of a fractured society requires long-term visions.

Before moving to the next stage, the achievement of some tasks serves as a critical condition for further progress. Complete or substantial disarmament is often considered necessary prior to conducting elections since that prevents the losers of the election from returning back to fighting. In Angola, the Uniao Nacional para a Independencia Total de Angola (UNITA)'s military strength and control of significant areas of territories gave the rebel forces an opportunity to refuse their defeat in the national election and re-initiate a civil war. The collapse of a peace process in Angola thus can be ascribed to failure in disarmament and demobilisation of combatants before elections, especially in the absence of confidence building between the two former adversaries.

In a peacebuilding context, a missed opportunity can refer to a moment when the failure of implementing certain measures within a given time frame results in a setback to the entire process or stop movement toward the next step. Overcoming the long history of animosity and mutual accusations can be easier during the early implementation stage when people still have great optimism (Cohn, 1999). It is costly to miss the moment when all the parties have devotion and hope for future cooperation following the euphoria of peace agreements. More time consuming negotiations are inevitable to revitalise the peace process when the support for the cause of peace evaporates. The failure of timing in transforming post-conflict dynamics has proven devastating in the continued cycle of violence in Angola and Sierra Leone (*The Economist*, 2000).

Actors and Levels

For the effective implementation of a peace plan, co-ordination among various parties has to be based on synchronisation of strategies at different levels (inter-personal, group and society). Activities, which are regarded as appropriate at one level, can have either a positive or negative impact on other levels. Reconciliation programmes designed for social rehabilitation and community building can be supported by and have a positive impact on healing at an individual level. On the other hand, community level reconciliation designed for control of ethnic violence would not be effective without the cooperation of national elites in mitigating ethnic hatred. Elections conducted to restore political institutions at a national level, as we have seen in Bosnia, can actually deepen ethnic divisions at a community level (Shoup, 1997). Major changes would not be achieved just by political compromise at the top level but have to reflect concerns at the grassroots level.

Peace initiatives can be taken at any level, as we have seen, for instance, in UNESCO projects on peace culture in El Salvador and other divided societies as well as grassroots projects organised out of local necessities. It is important to identify prime actors at different levels who demonstrate a commitment to a peace process (European Centre for Conflict Prevention, 1999). At an operational level, multiple and complex relationships exist among various types of actors, including aid recipients and providers; local authorities and international agencies; local residents and returnees. The role of health officials and refugee camp leaders (who carry out relief projects) differs from that of the political and military elites who are mostly detached from local situations.

The analysis of relationships among actors includes a formal top elite level network and their relationships to the grassroots (Lederach, 2001). Those serving the needs of local communities and indigenous non-governmental organisations have different agendas from those of politicians and diplomats. One of the key tasks is to find a critical mass of groups in support of peacebuilding in order to counterbalance the old warlords. External intervention is inevitable in the absence of indigenous mechanisms to control continuing ethnic tension (Abiew, 2000). The support of external actors is critical in stabilising short-term crisis management through peacekeeping or conflict resolution (de Geoffroy, 1999). Donors may promise funds as incentives to induce behavioural changes. External intervention is planned as temporary, and given the inevitability of eventual disengagement, foreign aid can be more focused on capacity building initiated by local actors.

Challenges lie in how external actors establish their relationships with local communities. Advocacy roles are more important than passive neutrality in enhancing human rights or economic conditions. For instance, improvement in human rights in places like Cambodia would not be possible without external pressure (Doyle, 1995). At the same time, external actors have a limited capacity to bring about peaceful changes if the local population does not support their moral authority.

Balance in the roles among local actors and intervenors has to be reversed at a more mature stage of peacebuilding. Both political and logistical considerations have an impact on the duration of the intervention and timing regarding when foreign aid should start and end. Sustainability is an important criterion in determining the reduced role and a terminating point for external support. Exit strategies have to focus on how the withdrawal of external presence would affect dynamics in the relationship between local parties.

EVALUATING THE PROCESS AND OUTCOME

Peace settlements have not been sufficiently sustainable in several noticeable situations. In other situations, high levels of violence may have been controlled, but many unresolved issues have re-generated confrontation. In Cambodia and Liberia, the establishment of new governments did not markedly improve social and political conditions. In most cases, the record of compliance with the agreed peace accord is seen as mixed. In El Salvador, Namibia, Mozambique and other relatively successful cases, reconciliation, social and economic reform muddled through.

In evaluating the outcome, both objective and subjective criteria need to be synthesised. Objective criteria assess direct and tangible outcomes in political, economic and social arenas. Subjective criteria, based on perceptions and expectations, are indirect and thus not easily quantifiable or tangible. They focus on psychological, cultural and spiritual dimensions of transition to peace. Progress in such targets as the number of returned refugees or increasing economic productivity can be numerically reported across cases (Jeong, 1999). On the other hand, it is important to recognise that non-material, human elements are not easy to calculate, and that some kinds of value judgments are inevitably involved in assessing a peace process and outcome.

Not every peace process is a linear phenomenon, and can be easily derailed. Measuring progress and its sustainability remains the most challenging question because it is not be easy to find a clear agreement on what kind of time frame and criteria should be used. Since many qualitative factors cannot be measured mechanically, evaluating the outcome is rather elusive and subject to interpretation. Thus, success becomes a relative concept (Pugh, 2000).

Policy options can also be considered in terms of intended and unintended outcomes. The processes of democratisation and economic development can bring about unintended outcomes such as monopoly of power by one dominant ethnic group and unequal distribution of wealth respectively. In El Salvador and Nicaragua, human development agendas have been undermined by monetary and other macro-economic policies (which were prescribed by Western donors as conditions for an aid) while these policies were originally designed to control inflation and reduce government deficit.

Progress should be measured on different dimensions, and can be compared with other cases in the context of their overall impact on the process. While political arrangements and local ethnic relations differ, the past and current phases of rebuilding Kosovo and Bosnia can be meaningfully compared. In addition, even though the impact of a third party intervention on local dynamics is not the same, Bosnia and Somalia can be contrasted in terms of the complexities of state building (Adam et al., 1998; Jan, 2001; Vuckovic, 1999). Analysis based on time progression can be used to examine various cases according to how long it has taken to accomplish the same or similar tasks. Difficulties in achieving the goals have to be judged by looking at the degree of challenges facing each case.

CONCLUSION

In order to avoid high human costs of failed transition to a stable society, a systematic approach is required. It is important to develop clear sets of agreed norms and expectations among various groups in formulating coherent approaches to peacebuilding. There is also a great demand for linkage and co-ordination of separate functions that otherwise may not be compatible with each other. On the other hand, peace implementation is full of contradictions, as exemplified by compromise between the pursuit of justice and political reality. Designing a peacebuilding process is not only a science, but also an art in the sense that imagination and creativity are essential parts.

REFERENCES

H. M. Adam, R. Ford and A. J. Ahmed, *Removing Barricades in Somalia: Options for Peace and Rehabilitation* (Washington, D.C.: United States Institute of Peace, 1998).

M. J. Anstee, *Orphan of the Cold War: The Inside Story of the Collapse of the Angolan Peace Process* (New York: St. Martin's Press, 1996).

M. L. Baregu, *Preventive Diplomacy and Peace-Building in Southern Africa* (Harare: SAPES Trust, 1999).

A. Bernardo and C. Ortigas, *Building Peace: Essays on Psychology and the Culture of Peace* (Manila: De La Salle University Press, 2000).

S. Byrne and L. Keashly, 'Working with Ethno-political Conflict: a Multi-Modal Approach', in T. Woodhouse and O. Ramsbotham (eds), *Peacekeeping and Conflict Resolution* (London: Frank Cass, 2000).

A. Cana and H. Dada, 'Political Transition and Institutionalization in El Salvador', in C. Arnson (ed.), *Comparative Peace Processes in Latin America* (Washington, D.C.: Woodrow Wilson Center Press, 1999), pp. 69-96.

J. Cockell, 'Conceptualising Peacebuilding: Human Security and Sustainable Peace', in M. Pugh (ed.), *Regeneration of War-torn Societies* (New York: St. Martin's Press, 2000), pp. 15-34.

I. Cohn, 'Post-conflict Programming: Feelings Fatigue', *UN Chronicle*, vol. 36, no. 2 (1999), pp. 36-37.

V. de Geoffroy, 'What Role for the Military in Rehabilitation', in C. Pirotte, et al. *Responding to Emergencies and Fostering Development: The Dilemmas of Humanitarian Aid* (London: Zed Books, 1999), pp. 154-157.

M. Doyle, *UN Peacekeeping in Cambodia: UNTAC's Civil Mandate* (Boulder: Lynn Rienner, 1995).

M. Doyle and N. Sambanis, 'International Peacebuilding: A Theoretical and Quantitative Analysis', *The American Political Science Review*, vol. 94, no. 4 (2000).

The Economist, 'Peacekeeping Disaster in Sierra Leone', vol. 355, no. 8169 (2000).

European Centre for Conflict Prevention, International Fellowship of Reconciliation, and State of the World Forum, *Peace Building Peace: 35 Inspiring Stories from Around the World* (Netherlands: Otto Harrassowitz, 1999).

R. J. Fisher, 'Social-Psychological Processes in Interactive Conflict Analysis and Reconciliation', in H. W. Jeong (ed.), *Conflict Resolution: Dynamics, Process and Structure* (Aldershot: Ashgate, 1999), pp. 81-104.

T. Franck, 'A Holistic Approach to Building Peace', in Olara Otunnu (ed.), *Peacemaking and Peacekeeping for the New Century* (Lanham: Rowman & Littlefield Publishers, 1998).

J. Goodhand and D. Hulme, 'NGOs and Peacebuilding in Complex Political Emergencies: An Introduction', Working Paper (Institute for Development Policy Management, University of Manchester, 1997).

G. Harris, 'Peacebuilding and Reconstruction after War in Developing Countries', *The Journal of Interdisciplinary Economics*, vol. 10 (1999), pp. 107-122.

D. Holiday and W. Stanley, 'Under the Best Circumstances: ONUSAL and the Challenges of Verification and Institution Building in El Salvador', in T. S. Montgomery (ed.), *Peacemaking and Democratization in the Western Hemisphere* (Coral Gables: North-South Center Press, University of Miami, 2000).

A. Jan, 'Somalia: Building Sovereignty or Restoring Peace?' in E. M. Cousens, et al. (eds), *Peace Building as Politics* (Boulder: Lynne Reinner, 2001).

H. W. Jeong, 'Peacebuilding in Identity Driven Ethnopolitical Conflicts', in S. Byrne, et al. (eds), *Conflict in Divided Societies: Theory and Applications* (Bloomfield: Kumarian Press, 2000).

H. W. Jeong, 'Epistemological Foundations for Peace Research', in J. P. De Cuellar, Honorary Editor-in-Chief; J. S. Sohn, Editor-in-Chief, *The World Encyclopedia of Peace*, vol. II (New York: Oceana Publications, Inc., 1999).

S. Jonas, 'Between Two World: the United Nations in Guatemala', in T. S. Montgomery (ed.), *Peacemaking and Democratization in the Western Hemisphere* (Coral Gables: North-South Center Press, University of Miami, 2000).

H. C. Kelman, 'Social-psychological Contributions to Peacemaking and Peacebuilding in the Middle East', *Applied Psychology*, vol. 47, no. 1 (1998).

C. Knox and P. Quirk, *Peace Building in Northern Ireland, Israel and South Africa: Transition, Transformation and Reconciliation* (Houndmills: Macmillan, 2000).

F. Kofi Abiew, 'Outside Agents and the Politics of Peacebuilding and Reconciliation', *International Journal*, vol. 55, no. 1 (2000).

R. Kraybill, 'Principles of Good Process Design', in L. Reychler and T. Paffeholz (eds), *Peacebuilding: A Field Guide* (Boulder: Lynne Rienner, 2000), pp. 173-183.

L. Kriesberg, 'Path to Varieties of International Reconciliation', in H. Jeong (ed.), *Conflict Resolution: Dynamics, Process and Structure* (Aldershot: Ashgate, 1999), pp. 105-130.

C. Kumar, 'Somalia: Building Sovereignty or Restoring Peace?' in E. M. Cousens, et al. (eds), *Peace Building as Politics* (Boulder: Lynne Rienner, 2001).

J. P. Lederach, 'Beyond Violence: Building Sustainable Peace', in E. Weiner (ed.), *The Handbook of Interethnic Coexistence* (New York: Continuum, 1998).

J. P. Lederach, *Building Peace: Sustainable Reconciliation in Divided Societies* (Tokyo: UN University Press, 1994).

J. P. Lederach, 'Levels of Leadership', in L. Reychler and T. Paffeholz (eds), *Peacebuilding: A Field Guide* (Boulder: Lynne Rienner, 2000), pp. 145-156.

P. P. Lizee, *Peace, Power and Resistance in Cambodia: Global Governance and the Failure of International Conflict Resolution* (New York: St. Martin's Press, 1999).

M. Lumsden, 'Breaking the Cycle of Violence', in H. W. Jeong (ed.), *Conflict Resolution: Dynamics, Process and Structure* (Aldershot: Ashgate, 1999), pp. 131-152.

M. Lund, 'A Toolbox for Responding to Conflicts and Building Peace', in L. Reychler and T. Paffenholz (eds), *Peacebuilding: A Field Guide* (Boulder: Lynne Rienner, 2001), pp. 16-20.

V. Magolin and R. Buchanan (eds), *The Idea of Design* (Cambridge: The MIT Press, 1998).

A. Malaquias, 'The UN in Mozambique and Angola: Lessons Learned', in J. Ginifer (ed.), *Beyond the Emergency: Development within UN Peace Missions* (London: Frank Cass, 1997), pp. 87-103.

R. Mani, 'The Rule of Law or the Rule of Might? Restoring Legal Justice in the Aftermath of Conflict' in M. Pugh (ed.), *Regeneration of War-torn Societies* (New York: St. Martin's Press, 2000), pp. 90-111.

K. Maynard, 'Rebuilding Community: Psychological Healing, Reintegration, and Reconciliation at the Grassroots Level', in K. Kumar (ed.), *Rebuilding Societies After Civil War: Critical Roles for International Assistance* (Boulder: Lynne Rienner, 1997).

H. Miall, et al., *Contemporary Conflict Resolution: The Prevention, Management and Transformation of Deadly Conflicts* (Cambridge: Polity Press, 1999).

C. Montiel, 'Toward a Psychology of Structural Peace Building', in D. Christie et al. (eds), *Peace, Conflict and Violence* (Upper Saddle River: Prentice Hall, 2001), pp. 282-294.

R. Orr, 'Building Peace in El Salvador: From Exception to Rule', in E. M. Cousens, et al. (eds), *Peace Building as Politics* (Boulder: Lynne Reinner, 2001).

S. Patrick, 'The Donor Community and the Challenge of Postconflict Recovery', in S. Forman and S. Patrick (eds), *Good Intentions: Pledges of Aid for Postconflict Recovery* (Boulder: Lynn Rienner, 2000).

M. Popkin, *Peace without Justice: Obstacles to Building the Rule of Law in El Salvador* (University Park: Pennsylvania State University Press, 2000).

M. Pugh, 'Introduction: the Ownership of Regeneration and Peacebuilding', in M. Pugh (ed.), *Regeneration of War-torn Societies* (New York: St. Martin's Press, 2000), pp. 1-12.

S. R. Ratner, *The New UN Peacekeeping: Building Peace in Lands of Conflict After the Cold War* (Basingstoke: Macmillan, 1995).

L. Reychler, 'Peace Architecture', Paper presented at the International Peace Research Association (Helsinki, August 2000a).

L. Reychler, 'Conceptual Framework', in L. Reychler, L. and T. Paffeholz (eds), *Peacebuilding: A Field Guide* (Boulder: Lynne Rienner, 2000b), pp. 3-15.

P. Shoup, 'The Elections in Bosnia and Herzegovina: The End of an Illusion', *Problems of Post-Communism*, vol. 44, no. 1 (January-February 1997).

R. S. Silver, *Promoting Democracy in Postconflict Societies: An International Dialog* (Washington, D.C.: Center for Development Information and Evaluation, U.S. Agency for International Development, 1999).

S. J. Stedman and D. Rothchild, 'Peace Operations: From Short-Term to Long-Term Commitment', in Jeremy Ginifer (ed.), *Beyond the Emergency: Development within UN Peace Missions* (London: Frank Cass, 1997), pp. 17-35.

C. Thayer, 'United Nations Transitional Authority in Cambodia: the Restoration of Sovereignty', in Tom Woodhouse et al. (eds), *Peacekeeping and Peacemaking: Towards Effective Intervention in Post-Cold War Conflicts* (Houndsmills: Macmillan, 1998).

United Nations Department for Economic and Social Information and Policy Analysis, *An Inventory of Post-Conflict Peace-Building Activities* (New York: United Nations, 1996).

G. Vuckovic, 'Promoting Peace and Democracy in the Aftermath of the Balkan War: Comparative Assessment of the Democratization and Institution-Building Processes in Croatia, Bosnia and Herzegovina, and Former Yugoslavia', *World Affairs*, vol. 162, no. 1 (1999), pp. 3-11.

B. F. Walter, 'Designing Transitions from Civil War: Demobilisation, Democratization, and Commitments to Peace', *International Security*, no. 24 (Summer 1999).

E. J. Wood, *Foreign Democracy from Below: Insurgent Transitions in South Africa and El Salvador* (Cambridge: Cambridge University Press, 2000).

8 Operational Issues for Peacebuilding: Organisational Imperatives

Ho-Won Jeong and David Last

In order to be effective, the work of various organisations has to be embedded in the overall peacebuilding plan. Since commitment and resources are usually less than desired, success depends on co-ordination and teamwork. Thus improved planning and effective co-ordination are crucial for successful peace operations.

Multi-component peacebuilding programmes require both vertical and horizontal co-ordination among a large number of organisations, which have diverse responsibilities. In a multi-functional mission, with geographical dispersion, there is always a danger of miscommunication if each component reports only to its central headquarters without lateral contact at every level. Since various components of peacebuilding missions often work in the same theatre of operation in isolation and against each other, horizontal co-ordination is critical for promoting the collaboration of actions among organisations.

'The co-ordination of activities within a mission presupposes a certain unity of command to ensure that a coherent strategy is consistently carried out' (Mockaitis, 1999, p. 135). But unity of command is impossible when there are many autonomous organisations at work. International organisations like the Organisation for Security and Cooperation in Europe (OSCE), North Atlantic Treaty Organization (NATO) and the UN cannot submit easily to external command. Nor do self-mandated NGOs with responsibilities to their charters and their donors. They must therefore find ways to work together within a mission framework.

This entails understanding the mandates and limitations of organisations around them and finding mechanisms to share information and organise their work. This chapter examines how various components of peacebuilding programmes in different sectors can be co-ordinated. We begin by considering the responsibilities of the international organisations now engaged in post-conflict reconstruction in general. We then consider some of the co-ordination mechanisms at work in the complex theatre of Bosnia. Finally, we offer examples of work in peacebuilding aimed at overcoming 'implementation gap'. While large international agencies have management and organisational skills, they often lack the psycho-social and cultural skills of the small NGOs with local partners. These are the crucial component for sustainable peacebuilding at the community level.

ORGANISATIONAL RESPONSIBILITIES AND CO-ORDINATION

The earliest UN observer missions and special commissions (such as the United Nations Truce Supervision Organisation in Israel/Palestine, 1948) combined military observation and the diplomatic functions of the special envoy. When forces were deployed after 1956 under military commanders in Egypt, Cyprus and the Congo, diplomatic 'peacemaking' functions were either conducted outside the theatre by special envoys, or conducted by the force commander with a political advisor, within the scope of the military mandate (James, 1990). The first Special Representative of the Secretary General (SRSG) was appointed to the UN Yemen Observation Mission (UNYOM) in 1963.

Since then, the relations between military and civilian mission components have varied, but the UN Transition Assistance Group (UNTAG) in Namibia saw the first attempt to give the SRSG an overarching role in co-ordination of the military and civilian elements of the mission (United Nations, 1996). In complex operations where there is a threat to international peace and security, the SRSG plays a critical role in providing political direction in the field. The Special Representative can have 'full responsibility for negotiating and implementing the peace process, managing the input of the UN Secretariat, mobilising the support of the operational funds and programmes for humanitarian and development activities and leading the team of autonomous specialised agencies' (Whaley, 1997, p. 116). Therefore, the SRSG should have the ability to effectively manage complex organisations and mobilise resources and public support as well as possessing negotiation and political skills.

Martti Ahtisaari, SRSG for the UN Transition Assistance Group in Namibia, was overseeing the mission's planning and subsequent implementation. While his main task was to be in charge of three thousand and five hundred civilians, of which close to half were hired for the civilian police force, he also helped set up the establishment of a joint working group on political problems. In the work of monitoring and preventing violence, the network of district officers supported the SRSG by reporting about political development. By informing local people as to the nature of the UN Namibia mandate, he was able to obtain support of the local population for the legitimacy of UNTAG.

While the Namibia mission is considered one of the most successful post-conflict peacebuilding operations, the SRSG has not always been able to draw political, civil and military elements together into a common approach. In practice, the role and power of the Special Representative are affected by external support and leadership qualities. Aldo Ajello, SRSG in the UN mission to Mozambique (1992-1994), enjoyed more authority over the control of local situations through chairing supervisory and monitoring commissions than the Special Representative in Angola Margaret Anstee. Despite a great need for more international intervention, the Second UN Angola Verification Mission (UNAVEM) II (1991-1995) was not able to go beyond observing and verifying the national elections with a limited number of personnel and resources, in part, because international attention was devoted to other operations.

Successful co-operation requires the proper allocation of resources, which are commensurate to the complexity of the tasks. Compared with the Namibia mission, the UN civil administration in Cambodia established in February 1992 had more difficult challenges with its expansion to a comprehensive settlement, including civil and electoral administration, repatriation, rehabilitation and protection of human rights. All these tasks had to be accomplished by fewer than 200 inexperienced staff recruited to cover civil administration activities for both central and regional offices. While the UN eventually took full responsibility for the conduct of the poll (Findlay, 1995), the UN Transition Authority in Cambodia (UNTAC) was not able to come up with more concerted efforts to resolve post-election political disputes.

When the local administration is in disarray (as it was in Somalia), an operation may be authorised by an international mandate to exercise more direct control. UN observers might set up and monitor local authority. The international mission also may assume authority to re-direct local policy decisions and even dismiss personnel. On the other hand, not every mission is required to have direct control over local situations, and most missions are more oriented toward assisting national authorities than replacing them. International operations can also adopt a partnership arrangement in establishing an international standard for the development of government structures.

Many missions have divisions on elections, human rights, humanitarian relief and development as well as the military and police components. A Resident Co-ordinator may be appointed (before or after a security crisis) to co-ordinate UN programmes. The co-ordinator may be drawn from a wide range of UN bodies and helps to organise more coherent UN activities in development areas at a country level. Given their expertise in development planning, the Resident Representatives of United Nations Development Programme (UNDP) are particularly well placed to ensure the focus of the work in countries that need development assistance. In recognition of its traditional work to protect refugees, the United Nations High Commission for Refugees (UNHCR) has been designated as a lead agency for assistance to war victims. The Resident Co-ordinator can serve as deputy to the SRSG for humanitarian and development activities (Whaley, 1997). The Resident Co-ordinator's role is a useful mechanism to counter the pressures for fragmentation and help the transition between development and security crises. Co-ordination issues become complicated, since many organisations tend to go beyond their competence in particular areas with the development of dual mandates in other areas. For instance, the UNDP and UNICEF have long-term social and economic development goals, but they have recently been involved in relief work, too, which addresses short-term humanitarian emergencies. At the same time, development agencies begin to pay more attention to fostering human rights with a focus on long-term social needs.

The maximisation of efforts often fails because many organisations take simultaneous actions to achieve opposing goals (Whitman and Bartholomew, 1994). Incompatibilities between activities derive from different organisational goals, values and cultures. Funds to cover large expenses for reconstruction, land transfer, demobilisation, judicial, military and police reform need to be mobilised by international financial institutions through donor meetings. At the same time, fiscal constraints often imposed by IMF austerity programmes put pressure on the local population while attempting to tackle monetary and budgetary issues. A programme on macro-economic stability needs to be counterbalanced with projects, which focus on micro level initiatives.

Economic and social reconstruction cannot be co-ordinated through a clear chain of command, which is common in war zones. Centralisation will not happen since various international agencies and NGOs want to keep autonomy and resist any attempts to impose external authority over them (Weiss, 1999). Since co-ordination has to be based on consensus, leadership lies in the capacity to orchestrate a coherent response and mobilise the key actors around common objectives and set up priorities.

The domain of activity and the level of organisational hierarchy are two variables affecting the extent to which actors are engaged in co-ordination. In the absence of an effective co-ordinating entity, the rudimentary exchange of information can be achieved through regular briefing sessions. The compatibility of field activities can be promoted by the negotiation of inter-agency frameworks for action with the establishment of task teams on specific issues. Clear structures for co-ordination among key agencies are essential for supporting the division of labor among actors.

ORGANISATIONAL LINKS AND LEVELS OF OPERATION: BOSNIA AND HERZEGOVINA

Bosnia-Herzegovina is particularly rich in the number and variety of programmes designed for post-conflict reconstruction. In that sense, Bosnia-Herzegovina is a laboratory for applying new understandings of peacebuilding to overcoming local challenges (Bosco, 1998). Co-ordination in Bosnia and Herzegovina is very complex due to heavy presence of international organisations with different mandates. With the involvement of the UN, NATO and OSCE, there are multiple layers of authorities and responsibilities divided among different agencies for governance, security, relief, development and economic recovery.

Separating the complex international intervention into 'levels of operation' can be a useful device. At the 'strategic' level, organisations make decisions about their objectives. In the case of the UN, this happens in New York with some decisions delegated to the mission in Sarajevo. The same thing can be said about the relationship between Brussels and Sarajevo for NATO missions. Most large NGOs have headquarters outside Bosnia which set their strategic priorities. At the operational level, resources are matched to tasks in order to achieve objectives. Some operational decisions are made centrally; others are delegated to regional offices such as one of the three UN and military regions that report to the Sarajevo headquarters. Finally, at the 'tactical' level for soldiers or at the community level for NGOs, people carry out specific tasks like patrolling or delivering food parcels.

The High Representative appointed by the Peace Implementation Council is responsible for implementation of civilian aspects of the operation, but he cannot work in isolation. The authority of the SRSG is limited to the supervision of functions carried out by the UN Mission in Bosnia-Herzegovina (UNMIBH): human rights, some civil administration functions, demining and policing. On the other hand, the OSCE is the lead organisation for democratisation, elections, confidence-building and inter-entity institutions. Most third-party military security functions are implemented by NATO's Stabilisation Force (SFOR), while development issues have become a main focus of UNDP, UNICEF and other UN Specialised Agencies.

Co-ordinating Authorities

The High Representative (HR) selected by Western powers has the final authority regarding interpretation of the peace agreement on civilian implementation such as the return of displaced persons and refugees, humanitarian assistance and the election process. The administrative Office of the High Representative (OHR) is also involved in the co-ordination of economic reconstruction, social rehabilitation, political and legal affairs and the promotion of human rights.

If public officials of the entities fail to comply with the Dayton Peace Agreement, the High Representative is given authority to dismiss them or impose decisions. The High Representative has dismissed several federation officials and issued decisions amending federation laws on fund management and employment over the last five years. However, international authority has been challenged by nationalist elites whose power depends on the resistance to any change in the gains they obtained during wartime.

In particular, dealing with the military and political organisations in the Croatian part of Bosnia has proved to be a critical test. They exercise direct control over the local communities through taxation and confiscation of production facilities. The European Union Administration's attempt to reorganise the administrative district in Mostar was met by resistance from Croats. Difficulties in the control of extreme elements (which challenge the decisions of the High Representative) have delayed the peace implementation process. As recently as spring 2001, a nationalist Croat group used rioters to block the investigation of the banks controlled by a Croatian nationalist party (*The Washington Post*, April 6). A lack of effective political pressure on the Croatian government (which can influence the local groups) by Western governments weakened the position of the High Representative.

The Special Representative of the Secretary General, as head of the United Nations Operations in Bosnia and Herzegovina, exercises authority over the three major components of United Nations Mission in Bosnia and Herzegovina (UNMIBH), including the United Nations International Police Task Force (IPTF), Civil Affairs and the Mine Action Center. The Special Representative also co-ordinates other UN activities in the areas of humanitarian relief and refugees, human rights, elections and rehabilitation of infrastructure and economic reconstruction. In addition, the office organises inter-agency meetings on a monthly basis to exchange information and co-ordinate overall UN activities with those of other international actors, especially the OHR.

Bosnia is a more complex peace building challenge than Cambodia where the UN was a single authority to supervise war termination. In Cambodia, institutional and structural simplicity of the mission was provided by the fact that the SRSG in Cambodia Yasushi Akashi was able to instruct and guide the overall peace process. In Bosnia, while major responsibilities to rebuild society belong to diverse international organisations, the OHR replaced the SRSG for the co-ordination function. However, the OHR lacked the directive authority of the SRSG in Cambodia; UN agencies and OSCE have autonomy for their own operations, as each has its own line of supervision.

Another major difference between Bosnia and Cambodia was that civilian and military operations were married under the UNTAC umbrella, but the two components were not integrated in Bosnia. In Cambodia, joint military-civil co-ordinating groups were established to successfully meet with the challenges of maintaining security and holding the elections despite the threats from the Khmer Rouge. UNTAC's military unit was assigned to high and medium risk areas to support electoral preparations. In the areas of lower risk, civilians were protected by unarmed civilian police and UN military observers. The major weakness in the Bosnian operation is the separation of NATO (which contributed the majority of forces to peacekeeping) from the civilian administrative function (Williams, 1999).

Democracy and Governance

The United Nations Mission in Bosnia and Herzegovina (UNMIBH) contributes to the establishment of the rule of law through a variety of programmes on reform and monitoring of the police and the judicial system. Police monitoring, training and assistance have been provided by the IPTF. The international police force was created to help the parties carry out their law enforcement responsibilities as set forth by the Peace Agreement. The institutions need to be restructured in order to create a democratic and professional police force. The international police mission has been making progress in establishing a truly multi-ethnic police force. The IPTF advised local police on providing security for returning refugees, and its training units addressed key public security issues such as organised crimes, drugs and corruption as well as refugee returns. Its executive power was extended to investigate allegations of human rights violations by police officers.

The UN Civil Affairs officers, deployed with their civilian police colleagues, monitor human rights, political and socio-economic situations. By providing information and analysis, they support the activities of the IPTF, SRSG and OHR. Alleged human rights violations are also investigated by officials at the OSCE Office for Democratic Institutions and Human Rights. They frequently meet with judges, prosecutors and lawyers. Their ultimate goal is to support the creation of an independent judiciary.

Along with bilateral projects like those of USAID's Office of Transition Initiatives, the OSCE has been interested in the development of civil society. Programmes on local NGO development and formation of political parties have often been implemented by the National Democratic Institute and other Western based NGOs. These programmes focus on promoting a participatory government and an increased role for women in the political arena as well as an emphasis on behavioural change with transmission of knowledge, skills and attitudes.

In the early years of the international intervention in Bosnia, tension sometimes arose between human rights and democracy activities even within the same agency due to their different skill sets and approaches. Whereas the OSCE needed to develop a working relationship with local authorities in promoting democratisation, it had to respond to complaints against local officials through its advocacy role for human rights work.

Elections are also the purview of the OSCE with the involvement of collaborative efforts by the IPTF, UNHCR and SFOR in registration and protection of voters. The elections without the return of refugees do not reflect the pre-war population distribution and institutionalise ethnic power imbalance. Minority returns are thus linked to municipal and local government elections, since the elections conducted without the fair reflection of the original population can contribute to legitimising the outcome of ethnic cleansing.

Security and Enforcement Functions

The General Framework Agreement for Peace (GFAP) entrusts SFOR with maintaining order. SFOR deters a resumption of hostilities, provides selective support for civilian organisations, oversees de-militarisation and also pursues war criminals indicted by the International Criminal Tribunal for the Former Yugoslavia. The IPTF is limited to monitoring and training functions by its mandate without the authority to arrest or detain. Working closely with the IPTF at the community level, SFOR has been called upon to enforce IPTF directives or decisions of the OHR. Sometimes these decisions on enforcement have been taken at the highest level (the High Representative's meeting of Group Principals -- the senior authorities for each organisation). On other occasions, limited enforcement action in the case of inter-communal violence has been within the authority of the local SFOR commanders.

In response to concerns regarding a lack of effective communication between civilian administrators and military commanders, personnel with backgrounds in law enforcement, public health, communications, education and transportation have been deployed with the troops to improve cooperative relations with the OHR, OSCE and UNHCR (Williams, 1998). SFOR (and its precursor, the Implementation Force abbreviated as IFOR) gave tactical support to the OSCE in the logistical aspects of the operation such as transporting ballot boxes to polling stations.

On the other hand, military forces have sometimes been reluctant to support human rights and other agencies engaged in law enforcement functions (Cousens, 2001). The War Crimes Tribunal (whose operation largely depends on assistance of enforcement forces) expressed frustration about a lack of effective action by SFOR to arrest persons indicted for war crimes. Some national units of SFOR did not actively prevent local parties from interfering with freedom of movement supported by the UNHCR. Many nations' troops have been accused at times of failing to break up hostile crowds gathering to restrict movement or harass returnees. On the other hand, it can also be said that these are difficult accusations to assess because troops must act within their capabilities as well as within their mandate. It is apparent, however, that wherever physical insecurity persists, the success of the civilian aspects of peacebuilding relies on military support.

Civil-military cooperation centres can fulfill co-ordination functions with local and international civilian personnel. Although unified command is difficult to achieve in practice, an effective system of military and civil cooperation at all levels, from strategic to tactical, is essential for successful operation. Since the UNHCR requires more support of the military components than other civilian agencies, a contact relationship between the UNHCR and SFOR has been established not only at a headquarter level through the Combined Joint Civil Military Task Force but also at branch and field office levels.

Relief and Reconstruction

Relief and development are managed by the UNHCR and UNDP respectively. The role of the UNHCR evolved during the course of the Balkan conflict. Its field division co-ordinated humanitarian assistance and refugee safety issues. In the early phases of the war, it focused on camp management, provision of food, shelter, hygiene and the movement of individuals and groups to safety. As the implementation of the Peace Agreement progressed, it spent more time on encouraging the return of refugees and support for vulnerable groups. In collaborating with NGOs, it provided psycho-social programmes for the general population, home-care and support for the elderly, the handicapped, traumatised and households with no income.

From 1992 onward, the UNHCR found itself responsible for large numbers of refugees in areas where services and infrastructure had been severely damaged by fighting. Cities like Sarajevo could not support large refugee communities, but there was pressure to provide for them within Bosnia. The International Management Group (IMG) was conceived as an umbrella which could bring large donors like the European Community Humanitarian Organisation (ECHO) together with consortia of NGOs and international organisations to meet basic refugee needs. The IMG's role was to focus reconstruction efforts by surveying infrastructure capacity, comparing it to pre-war levels and recommending priorities. In 1996, the IMG operated three offices in Croatia and five in Bosnia, employing both local and international staff. In 1998, the UNDP expanded its Bosnian operation to include regional offices, and the IMG began to close down over the next 18 months.

In recognition that a lack of income is a major barrier to refugee resettlement, the UNDP has a comprehensive approach to reconstruction/rehabilitation. Physical rehabilitation activities for shelter and social infrastructure are part of the community development efforts needed to promote social cohesion in the smooth integration of refugees and displaced people. These efforts complement the objectives of the UNHCR in the areas of community development and promotion of reconciliation. At the same time, a large emphasis is placed on capacity building for strengthening a social safety net and supporting increased responsibilities of local authorities for social services. In order to help the return and peaceful integration of Croat and Serb refugees and displaced persons in Western Slovenia, the UNDP and UNHCR collaborated on a rehabilitation and reconstruction project with distribution of basic agricultural equipment and reconstruction of schools and roads.

UNHCR protection and field officers lack resources to deal with a large number of inter-personal and inter-communal problems. An effective response depends on several organisations. The UNHCR gets reports from OSCE human rights officials. Housing projects for returnees are supported by the UNDP. The IPTF and SFOR help ensure the safety of returning refugees (Whitman, 1999). The UNHCR also relies on other agencies to identify new returnees when it has low presence in local areas. Their programmes are implemented at a community level through contracts with NGOs.

Economic Recovery

Responsibility for economic recovery is split between international financial institutions and UN agencies. The World Bank and International Monetary Fund are responsible for aid co-ordination and have played a key role in financing Bosnia's reconstruction debt in collaboration with bilateral and private donors (Vayrynen, 1997). The UNDP has paid greater attention to income generating activities through emergency employment and the establishment of micro-enterprises, while private sector donors are more interested in industrial and commercial development.

Through reconstruction programmes, the UNDP supports reorganisation of essential municipal and social services and rehabilitation of basic infrastructure such as local roads, education, health, power and water supplies. The UNDP is also engaged in clearing the mined agricultural areas for farmers to cultivate. Recently the Resident Co-ordinator has taken the initiative to co-ordinate the preparation of a Common Country Study on main development challenges in Bosnia and Herzegovina aimed at fostering a common understanding among the agencies.

CO-ORDINATION MECHANISMS

Peacebuilding is a dynamic task, and we would expect co-ordination mechanisms to evolve over the course of a mission. Co-ordination mechanisms in Bosnia varied over time, but patterns can be found at the strategic, operational and tactical levels. It is consistently at the tactical level that we find niches that only NGOs can effectively fill.

In the early stages of planning a mission, most co-ordination begins at the top. NATO's North Atlantic Council and the UN Security Council, for example, negotiated memoranda of understanding about logistics and the responsibilities of each organisation before UNMIBH and IFOR were established. IFOR arrived in Bosnia first, and absorbed much of the command infrastructure of the UN Protection Force (UNPROFOR). NGOs had new priorities to deal with, and new areas to deploy into, but often found themselves dealing with the same military players during the transition period. One innovation at the strategic level in 1995 was the UN's invitation of NGOs to participate in weekly information sessions in New York with the Department of Humanitarian Affairs and the Department of Political Affairs. Interaction, as an umbrella organisation for more than a hundred American NGOs, participated in these meetings and disseminated information about ongoing UN missions to their members.

The figure (next page) illustrates the hierarchical relationships established in Bosnia after the Dayton agreement. Each organisation established a headquarters in Sarajevo and made some attempt to understand the objectives and methods of other organisations. In each case, however, the focus was understandably on their own task, and the organisation to which they were accountable: the Peace Implementation Council for the OHR; NATO for SFOR; UN headquartered in New York for UNMIBH. At the operational level, usually in the regional headquarters, resources and objectives had to be matched up. Here the incentives for cooperation were much greater. SFOR, IPTF and UNHCR held more frequent co-ordination meetings, exchanged liaison officers, and compared strategies before meeting with belligerent factions and local authorities.

Figure 1: Potential peacebuilders and the gap at the tactical level

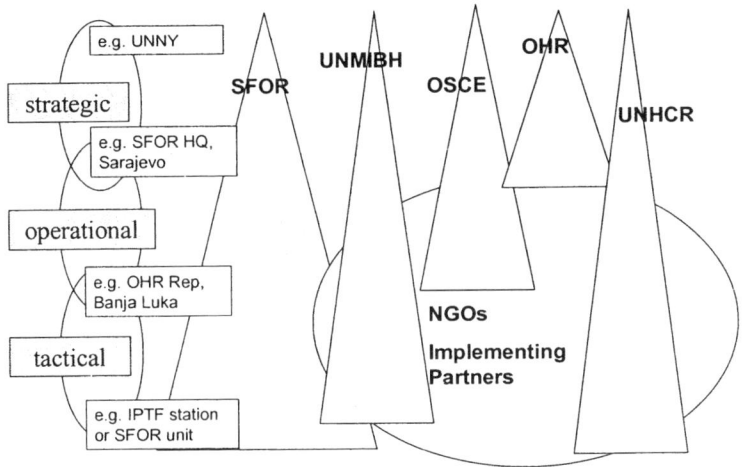

As the comparatively unified civil and military structure of UNPROFOR gave way to NATO, OHR, OSCE and UNMIBH, new forums were established for co-ordination. The organisations exchanged liaison officers to help explain themselves and keep informed about others' activities. A weekly meeting of 'Group Principals', which began in March 1996, was chaired by the High Representative and included SFOR commanders, SRSG, Commissioner of UN Civilian Police, and eventually encompassed representatives of the branch heads of the OSCE mission. OHR officials chaired many of the Joint Civil-Military Commissions established to supervise implementation of the annexed provisions of the GFAP.

A Joint Civil-Military Commission has at least three parts. One is the joint civil and military presence of the international third party. The other two parts are members of the belligerent communities (there may be three factions for some meetings in Bosnia). For any business to be done, the third party must facilitate communication between the opposing factions at the table. Often it is easier to get things done by shuttling between factions than having them at the same table. Three different kinds of meetings therefore occur at every level: meetings between members of the international community; meetings between members of the international community and one faction; and meetings with more than one faction. Meetings become increasingly difficult to prepare for and manage as the number of players increases.

By the time SFOR had separated the forces of the belligerent factions (120 days after the GFAP had been signed), JMCs chaired by soldiers were in place in each region down to the local or tactical level. Military commanders now had the problem of linking up with civil authorities, international organisations, and NGOs in their areas. By mid-1996, the UNMIBH and OSCE had regional headquarters in Mostar, Banja Luka and Brcko. Inter-agency cooperation was developed more quickly in these regional headquarters than in the politically sensitive atmosphere of Sarajevo.

At the operational level, the accomplishment of one agency's goal depends on the support of others and often requires their involvement in common tasks. Planning of security for returnees demands a field level consultation between the IPTF, local police, SFOR and UNHCR. A high level of collaboration of these agencies has proven critical to successful refuge returns. In Drvar, a town in Northwest Bosnia, the local UNHCR and OSCE officers co-ordinated their weekly activities with the IPTF and SFOR in order to handle an acute problem with Croat resistance to returns of Serb refugees. For local elections in the municipal area of Drvar, all the key international agencies were drawn together in meetings of the Election Results Implementation Committee.

Agreements at the regional level can be undermined by the inability of the higher headquarters of their respective organisations to determine a common policy. For example, in 1998, the UNHCR wanted to push for rapid return of refugees, but SFOR was concerned that this would destablise areas that were already tense and potentially violent. The result was a debacle in which the UNHCR encouraged returns in areas where the IPTF and SFOR could not ensure safety. In general, despite regular meetings, horizontal co-ordination in Sarajevo seems to be less effective than at a lower levels where regional offices are co-located.

An organisation's knowledge and ability to influence crisis situations depends on its local presence. SFOR has patrols at the village level. The IPTF has officers at municipal police stations. They share information with other organisations at the local and regional levels, and pass information up to the mission headquarters in Sarajevo. They can be directed to take action when things get out of hand on a street corner. As political organisations, the OSCE and OHR have some presence in regional headquarters, but neither organisation has a consistent presence in villages and communities. Initially limited to Sarajevo, the OHR engaged an NGO, the International Crisis Group (ICG), to provide it with some field officers at regional level. Although international field officers of the OSCE and OHR may have strong managerial, legal and policy implementation skills, the small number of officers, language barriers and cultural differences all limit their impact at the local level.

Civil-Military Cooperation (CIMIC) centres can fulfill co-ordination functions between military forces, local authorities and international civilian organisations. They work best at the local level. The role of a CIMIC centre evolves with the peacekeeping mission. In the early days of IFOR and SFOR, they were established at regional and local levels, and were concerned with humanitarian relief and assisting the deployment of other agencies. As the OSCE, IPTF and UN missions matured, CIMIC centres were less inclined to take their own initiatives, and were more involved in supporting the work of other international agencies.

In addition to CIMIC centers, exchanges of liaison officers, joint civil-military task forces and mixed civil-military working groups provide forums in which soldiers and civilians, locals and internationals can cooperate on specific issues. Election task forces (chaired by the OSCE), refugee repatriation task forces (chaired by UNHCR) and human rights working groups (chaired by UNHCR protection officers in the early stages of the mission) all worked at regional offices and down to the municipal level.

In all this co-ordination, however, there remained the problem of language and culture. At every level, but particularly at higher levels, the tendency was to cluster in international, English-speaking groups for co-ordination. While not immune to this tendency, NGOs did appear to be more engaged in the local community.

In general, organisations in charge of military and police missions reach all the way down to the tactical level. On the other hand, the OHR, OSCE and UNHCR heavily use implementing partners to put their programmes into effect because their operational functions do not penetrate effectively beyond regional offices. In addition, some service-oriented organisations find it difficult to set up a local infrastructure to implement their programmes in a short time. These agencies rely on NGO implementing partners to have a direct impact. The skills and structure to address communal conflict largely reside with NGOs.

PARTNERSHIP WITH NGOS

Since NGOs began to be hailed as being capable of bringing peace and development to war-torn societies through grassroots level activities, many NGOs have been given a contractual responsibility for specific programmes or activities as implementation partners. For example, the OHR contracted the International Crisis Group (ICG) to gather information and prepare reports. The OSCE democratisation branch works with local NGOs to develop civil society and build links between communities. As many NGOs often work as subcontractors, it is not unusual for NGOs to manage contracts for regional food deliveries or humanitarian services. On the other hand, some large international NGOs can set up priorities, raise and distribute their own resources rather than operating under the direct control of their government or UN agencies. The operational/tactical split between international agencies and NGOs has been particularly common for humanitarian relief and development work. In its co-ordinated scheme, many NGOs serve as sub-contractors who deliver specific goods and services. In running programmes to support its activities, the UNHCR contracts many of the basic services. NGO partners implementing UNHCR programmes provide packages for returnees who need to mend or re-build houses without roofs, windows or furniture and farmers stripped of tools, seed and livestock.

Some NGOs are engaged in working on unarmed accompaniment and assistance to returnees. When returnees face hostility, threats and intimidation, NGO members accompany them to their houses and assist them with repairs. The presence of an international witness helps deter threats and harassment. NGOs can provide information that allows IPTF or OSCE human rights officers to follow up on specific incidents. The United Methodist Committee on Relief (UMCOR), serving as a partner implementing UNHCR programmes, developed collaborative relationships with IPFT and SFOR in identifying new returnees in Northwestern Bosnia where they have low presence.

International organisations deal mainly with official government institutions, but have less contact with civil society. As discussed earlier, their capacity to collect and disseminate information and take action at the tactical level is enhanced by entering into partnership with NGOs. NGOs possess valuable information about the relative dependability of local groups and individuals and can easily establish logistics for various projects due to their long-standing relationship with local communities.

NGOs have unique advantages in the areas of civil society building through their conscious efforts to establish relationships between adversarial communities, foster mutual confidence and provide peaceful mechanisms of dispute resolution. 'Major international agencies tend to embody organisational skills, while therapeutic and psychosocial skills often reside in smaller NGOs'

(Last, 2000, p. 85). In promoting reconciliation, various NGO programmes have been active in strengthening inter-personal and inter-communal communication skills.

The substance of peacebuilding often hinges on conflict resolution skills, embedded in knowledge of the community. Owing to cultural and communication obstacles, the intervention of international staff is difficult at the community level. The same barriers also cause difficulties in developing plans at the operational level to support widespread action. Thus major international organisations develop or support local NGOs capable of carrying out projects in their own areas.

For instance, in the areas of reconciliation, the community centre model, with mixed local and international facilitators, provides a framework for deploying key inter-personal skills at the grass roots level. The networks of community groups can be established across ethnic boundaries to explore indigenous knowledge, skills and attitudes (Belloni, 2001). Both existing and potential groups, such as youth, women, pensioners, displaced people and refugees, can be organised at the grassroots level in certain geographic areas. They can be linked together at a regional level to permit broader understanding and pursue common interests.

In working with NGOs, flexibility in partnership arrangements is critical (Patrick, 2000). Donors should not insist too much on formal and institutionally verifiable goals on the part of any recipient operational body. Overall, the efficiency of small, operationally-oriented NGOs depends on a minimum administrative overhead without the necessity of a formal management structure. Especially in the areas of development and civil society building, hierarchical structures with links to central headquarters are less effective at developing appropriate local strategies. Nor is it desirable to manage and control NGOs that can operate autonomously within their mandates.

One group may get involved in overlapping areas of legal assistance, business development or psycho-social counseling, but diverse programmes have to serve shared goals since the limited pool of resources constrains the activities of each project. There may be an advantage to an integrated approach, for instance, by linking the provision of health care and development assistance to community reconciliation. Minority integration and return projects can be more effective when they are supported by health or legal assistance programmes. Community reconciliation, inter-cultural communication and education can be integrated into all aspects of social service programmes.

NGO WORK FOR COMMUNITY BUILDING

Peacebuilding initiatives are made more effective by a coherent campaign plan, which incorporates the skills of appropriate NGOs and uses their contacts at the grass roots level. Infrastructure building has to be closely linked to the 'social components' of confidence building and community organisation. Participation in public and volunteer works and informal contacts through neighbourhood programmes have been suggested as a means of increasing confidence within the community. The exchange of supplies and equipment between former enemies can lead to the development of common concerns affected by destruction.

Various professional sectors such as education, religion and social welfare can be adapted to community reconciliation programmes. Professional services in legal, health care and other areas have to promote the dignity of the victims, a climate of mutual understanding, tolerance and respect for different cultures. More attention needs to be paid to linking social service programmes to resolving tensions and disputes at an inter-group level.

Social and Legal Services for Refugee Return

Multiple agencies get involved in the mobilisation of resources for repairing houses as well as the prevention of vandalisation or looting. Rebuilding the communal links requires efforts to assist estranged neighbours to share apartment blocks or streets again. At the same time, counselling and physical protection have to be provided for displaced minorities who prepare for return. A comprehensive programme for a large-scale return of minorities has been supported by such international NGOs as Norwegian Refugee Council's Minority Integration and Return Project.

Advocate groups support and represent the rights of evicted elderly minority citizens and accompany their clients to local authorities. Legal assistance was provided for vulnerable pensioners, refugees and displaced people who had basic questions about their rights and how to pursue them. Since the returnees' rights are not compatible with the needs of displaced people or refugees occupying houses, support for population return at an operational level may be perceived as adversarial. Legal expertise is needed in such classified areas as property and occupancy rights, elections, pensions, family law, communal access and contracts.

Contradictory laws about property rights and procedures deprive many elderly pensioners and refugees of their homes or pensions. Movimiento por la Paz, el Desarme y la Libertad (MPDL), the Spanish NGO, hires local lawyers as advocates. Legal aides with minimal training fill out questionnaires to screen and sort the problems, then the lawyers provide advice, and sometimes represent clients in court, both in Banja Luka and within a day's drive. The MPDL is supported by the UNHCR as an implementing partner, assisting with return and resettlement.

The goal of reconciling interests and preferences at a personal level and rebuilding stable neighbourhood relationships cannot simply be achieved by enforcing eviction. The perception of minority groups as infiltrators should be reduced through community building projects. In order to understand complex social and inter-personal issues beyond legal classification, the assistance of social workers is needed. Local social workers help categorise various concerns such as repossession of former homes and other properties and non-discriminatory housing not only on legal but also social terms. This helps the MPDL implement psychosocial programmes for refugees and displaced people in Northwest Bosnia.

Health Care

Practical work to achieve health and welfare provides a context for sustained co-operation between communities. Humanitarian action in the field of health care can be designed to provide an incentive for continued engagement of formerly estranged communities with each other. Health Bridges for Peace is a project that supports the prevention of inter-communal conflict with health care programmes. It has been visible in several communities in the former Yugoslavia, and its activities were endorsed by the World Health Organisation. Health care delivery is combined with training in psychological skills as part of a conflict-management component.

In delivering primary health care, medical professionals representing diverse communities can develop inter-communal communication, promote trust and create avenues for the peaceful resolution of differences (Beigbeder, 1999). Through medical functions, the Medical Network for Social Reconstruction for ex-Yugoslavia advocates a model of inter-ethnic reconciliation and co-operation. The creation of training programmes across political and communal boundaries resulted in the establishment of 'Health and Reconciliation Teams'. Various service programmes implemented by foreign donors should support local programmes, which pursue the goal of overcoming ethnic or racial prejudice.

These legal, social and health programmes at the grass-roots level are examples of the sort of work which helps bridge the gap between large scale international intervention and sustainable peacebuilding at the community level. The latter cannot occur without the active involvement of members of the community with the language and cultural skills to engage their neighbours.

CONCLUSION

Peacebuilding activities in Bosnia require a secure environment as a starting point. Governance and democratisation, human rights, relief and development and long-term economic recovery all demand concerted international support. While co-ordination of activities at operational and tactical levels can be considered effective, more support for the OHR policies toward the corruption of Bosnian government officials and the nationalist Croat resistance to the efforts to establish a more integrated country is needed at the strategic level.

Agencies like the OSCE, UNHCR and OHR are increasingly relying on implementing partners to fill gaps at the tactical level. As peacebuilding progresses beyond relief and physical reconstruction, the pyscho-social and community organisation skills of local NGO partners will be increasingly important. The larger agencies will have to provide an inter-agency framework at each level that facilitates their work, because peacebuilding cannot progress without it.

Different expectations about the relationship make co-ordination among agencies difficult. Each international agency operates according to its own understanding of the situation, intervention policies and practice. Inter-agency dialogue is necessary for promoting mutual understanding of differences in organisational norms, values and beliefs as well as past practice. Inefficient co-ordination at higher levels can be compensated by focusing on building peaceful communities from the bottom up, where structures have the most impact on people's lives (Last, 2000).

REFERENCES

Y. Beigbeder, 'The World Health Organization and Peacekeeping', in J. Whitman (ed.), *Peacekeeping and the UN Agencies* (London: Frank Cass, 1999), pp. 31-48.

R. Belloni, 'Civil Society and Peacebuilding in Bosnia and Herzegovina', *Journal of Peace Research*, vol. 38, no. 2 (2001).

D. Bosco, 'After Genocide: Building Peace in Bosnia', *The American Prospect*, no. 39 (01 July 1998).

L. J. Cohen, 'Whose Bosnia? The Politics of Nation Building', *Current History*, vol. 97 (March 1998), pp. 103-112.

E. M. Cousens, 'Building Peace in Bosnia', in E. M. Cousens, et al. (eds), *Peace Building as Politics* (Boulder: Lynne Reinner, 2001), pp. 113-152.

T. Findlay, 'Cambodia: The Legacy and Lessons of UNTAC,' *SIPRI Research Report No. 9* (Oxford: Oxford University Press, 1995).

A. James, *Peacekeeping in International Politics* (London: Macmillan, 1990).

D. Last, 'Organizing for Effective Peacebuilding', in T. Woodhouse and O. Ramsbotham (eds), *Peacekeeping and Conflict Resolution* (London: Frank Cass, 2000), pp. 80-96.

D. Last, 'Implementing the Dayton Accords: the Challenges of Inter-Agency Co-ordination', in T. Woodcock (ed.), *Analysis of and for Conflict Resolution,* Proceedings of the Second Cornwallis Group Seminar, (Cornwallis, NS: Canadian Peacekeepers' Press, 1998), pp. 184-210.

T. R. Mockaitis, *Peace Operations and Intrastate Conflict: The Sword or the Oliver Branch?* (Westport: Praeger, 1999).

S. Patrick, 'The Donor Community and the Challenge of Postconflict Recovery', in S. Forman and S. Patrick (eds), *Good Intentions: Pledges of Aid for Postconflict Recovery* (Boulder: Lynn Rienner, 2000).

United Nations, *The Blue Helmets: A Review of United Nations Peacekeeping,* third edition (New York: United Nations Department of Public Information, 1996).

R. Vayrynen, 'Economic Incentives and the Bosnian Peace Process', in David Cortright (ed.), *The Price of Peace: Incentives and International Conflict Prevention* (Lanham: Rowman & Littlefield, 1997), pp. 150-180.

T. Weiss, *Military-Civilian Interactions: Intervening in Humanitarian Crises* (Lanham: Rowman & Littlefield, 1999).

J. D. Whaley, 'Improving UN Developmental Co-ordination within Peace Missions', in J. Ginifer (ed.), *Beyond the Emergency: Development within UN Peace Missions* (London: Frank Cass, 1997), pp. 107-122.

J. Whitman, 'The UN Specialized Agencies, Peacekeeping and the Enactment of Values', in J. Whitman (ed.), *Peacekeeping and the UN Agencies* (London: Frank Cass, 1999), pp. 120-137.

J. Whitman and I. Bartholomew, 'Collective Control of UN Peace Support Operations: A Policy Proposal,' *Security Dialogue,* vol. 25, no. 1 (1994), pp. 77-92.

M. C. Williams, 'Civil-Military Relations and Peacekeeping', *Adelphi Paper 321* (Oxford: Oxford University Press, 1998).

Index

Aid, 24, 28, 43, 62, 67-8, 70, 137, 157, 160-2
Afghanistan, 7
Africa, 9,35, 92-3, 108, 110, 112, 125-6, 130, 132, 137, 149, 151, 157
Angola, 4, 9, 18, 30, 32, 34-5, 63, 66, 152, 159, 173
Argentina, 108, 110
  Madres de la Plaza de Mayo, 108-9
Assessment, 8-9, 86, 91, 110, 148, 152
  design, 3, 11, 82-3, 147-163

Balkans, 62, 149
Bosnia-Herzegovina (BiH), 132, 176-7
Boulding, Elise, 135
Boutros-Ghali, Boutros, 20, 42, 64, 128
Buffer zone, 62, 68

Cambodia, 4, 9, 18, 30, 32, 36, 62-3, 65, 70, 73, 132, 149, 151, 153-4, 161, 174, 178
  Khmer Rouge, 4, 70
Capacity building, 3, 11, 92, 157, 161, 183
Capitalism, 26, 38, 40
Cease fire, 6, 21, 23, 62-4, 69, 75, 153, 157
Chile, 110
Civil-military cooperation centres, 181, 187
Civil-military operation team, 69
Civilian police (CIVPOL), 66, 72-3, 173, 178-9, 185
Cold War, 18, 19, 20, 25, 27-8, 62
Conflict
  management, 9, 65, 89, 97, 136, 159
  prevention, 73
  resolution,19, 24, 29, 64, 74, 82, 96, 129, 130, 134, 155, 161, 189
  transformation, 12, 115
Congo, Democratic Republic of, 19, 149, 172
Community building, 6, 11-12, 61, 67, 73-5, 133, 156-8, 160, 191-2
Croatia, 18, 44, 178, 182
Cyprus, 63, 74, 172

Dayton Peace Agreement, 177, 184
Demining, 63, 177
Demobilisation, 6, 18, 30, 63-4, 66, 85, 147, 152, 157, 159, 175
Democracy, 10, 25, 27, 29,